Living in Trauma

Acknowledgements

To Alex Benjamin, who trusted me to listen to him and tell his story. Alex went through some traumatic ordeals in life but he continued to rise. I am inspired by Alex's courage in the face of great suffering, pain and anxiety. When faced with real danger, threat of death as well as emotional and physical trauma Alex eventually began to seek help, to work towards healing and to breakdown internalised taboos around mental health. Some people may see Alex as a courageous young man, others may see him as stupid. Alex has been through some bittersweet experiences in life, time and time again he has faced and escaped death yet he is still with us undefeated. His story allows me to let people know that whatever your situation may be or how complicated your life is today, it can never determine what your tomorrow is going to look like.

It has not always been easy to deliver this piece, but it has always been important. Alex's story is a light in the darkness, a motivation for those who feel they should give up. I am truly grateful to Alex, for his time, his patience, openness, vulnerability and strength. It is a true honour to tell another human beings' story and to hopefully inspire others to find strength, to acknowledge their situation and to live a brighter day.

I am grateful to the Most High God for direction on the best way to deliver a tantalising story like this. Halloweth be thy name, my maker and the lover of my soul.

To my mother, my guilty pleasure. Your impartial love and selfless attributes made me achieve a lot in life, I'm always grateful for your encouragement and your support through this new milestone.

To my father, may your lovely soul rest in peace. His ideology about child-rearing was tough love. Although I didn't like it as a teenager, I can confirm he prepared his children for anticipated difficulties on our way to the top. He was a distinguished and principled high court judge who never compromised his beliefs until he gave up the ghost! Thanks for everything Pops!

To my siblings, we remind each other about our parents' lessons and stay together undivided. We have been able to maintain Father's legacy, and I am proud of all of you. Thanks for everything, and may your days be long.

To my late kid brother, I've been broken since you took that journey. The pain of your exit is what I have to live with for the rest of my life. You have left a permanent hole in the family but continue to rest on and I love you.

To my baby cousin, I was putting the manuscript together when I heard about your exit; your eldest brother called my mum to help break the news to your mum. My sister called me in tears because you were loved by all. You were a charismatic and vibrant fellow, and the future looked bright, but your life was cut short by an untimely death. You have just added to the traumatic baggage I'm carrying after losing pops and my little brother. Well, rest on and God knows best.

To the legendary Fela Anikulapo-Kuti, you fought for your people until you died. I am glad I was able to attend your Friday night jumps and experience your honest opinion about inequality. Some of your lessons were unclear then but are clearer now that I have seen the world. You were fearless and selfless. You put roofs over hundreds of people's heads and continued to fight against injustice. May you continue to rest in peace!

To my enemies, I thank you all for hating on me. Without your hatred and backbiting, I would not have gone for the bull's horn. You inspired me to want to do better in life; I thank you for your inspiration and motivation. God was present in my life from the moment I knew about my existence. He had my back and built walls of fire around me so that no weapon fashioned against me could prosper. He is a powerful and immortal entity who sits on his holy throne and controls heaven and earth.

Introduction

Living in Trauma is based on the true life experience of Alex Benjamin. Alex is a brave and courageous man whom I have known for decades. I find Alex's story very unusual, not only for its dramatic twists and turns but for the way in which Alex found help, continues to grow and evolve and how he refuses to be defined by the prejudice and misconceptions of others. I write Alex's story to explore different themes related to trauma and living in trauma. The themes move from the very intimate and personal, to religion, political structures, racism, xenophobia and stigma around mental health particularly among men.

Alex, like me, was born in Nigeria and now lives outside of the country. This is an important point to highlight as in an increasingly global and interconnected world our stories, traumas and lived experiences cross the borders and boundaries of not only physical spaces but also of mental perception barriers. To suffer from mental health challenges rooted in experienced traumas is one thing, to suffer in environments where it is taboo to show perceived weakness or vulnerability as a man is another thing.

I asked Alex for his permission to put this work together because I felt so many people could benefit from his bittersweet experiences. It is different when you are a magnet to drama and have been through dramatic experiences, some that ended a success and some that ended a failure. It is not the end of the world when you fail; it might be life trying to teach you a lesson. Lessons of this kind stay with you for the rest of your life. Some bitter lectures can leave you with post-traumatic stress.

How you manage such stresses as you carry on with your life is very important. You can choose to let it have a negative effect or a positive effect on you. We are the CEOs of our own lives, the masters of our own destinies; we are responsible for whatever we experience in life. Life can sometimes be kind to us and life can be cruel as well. It's the reason we always need to have proactive mechanisms to handle whatever life throws at us. I have come to realise the kind of vibration we pick from people determines the behaviour people perceive in us. Vibration is a kind of wave we pick up from people. If you are to succeed in life, you need to have a proactive mechanism for negative vibrations because it is a strength stealer!

All success in life is rooted in either luck or failure. If you begin with luck, you learn nothing but arrogance. However, if you begin with failure and learn to evaluate it, you also learn to succeed. Failure begets knowledge. Out of knowledge, you gain wisdom, and it's with wisdom that you can become truly successful. Illiteracy and lack of knowledge is becoming more dangerous by the day. People all over the world need to stay undefeated by illiteracy because it determines their perspective to what they see around them every day. Creativity is said to beget more creativity, and previous failures can help shape future success. Unfortunately, illiteracy begets barbarism.

We are divided by uneducated thoughts like xenophobia, cannibalism, racism, and tribalism. The level of deep hatred amongst racial cultures is very worrisome. Alex is lucky enough to be able to share with me his romance with death in the hands of xenophobes. He took an unusual route to the top of his game, and he experienced some cruelty to humanity from fellow human beings. He was a vulnerable, shy, complicated, and curious kid. He did things his way, he was in the habit of running away from home at the age of fourteen. His curiosity got the better of him as he tried to experience different things.

During his route to the top of his game, he experienced some inhumane cruel behaviour from people of the same racial background. He was very vocal about his experience in Ivory Coast during his quest to find a better life and to see the world. I remember asking him why he embarked on a risky journey like that as a teenager. He emphasised the respect people give successful people in contrast to the disrespect that comes to people with shambolic lives, and I totally agree with the statement. This book is full of controversy, scandal, demonic encounters, suspense, love and politics.

However, you will applaud his bravery for some of his solutions. He was bullied as a kid until he was a teenager. He was sexually abused at the tender age of nine, which led to him having meaningless coitus with numerous ladies. Although he's not proud of it, he told me his therapist confirmed it was the reason for his high sex drive. The positive thing is in the face of numerous traumatic experiences he kept his head up and gave his life a counterattack, just to insert some greatness into his life. This book will help people in the same shoes as Alex, and upcoming teenagers will understand that you can't always submit to acting on impulse. He suffers severe anxiety and he always tries to keep it under control, but when you sit with him for five minutes, you will notice the fact that he can't stay still.

Through the telling of Alex's story, I will also mention my political views about how greed made religion a political strategy for money launderers, fake prophets, and religious fracas. My research into the history of slavery in Africa and the use of Christian religion to control and lure people aboard slave ships has been illuminating and shocking to me.[1] The parallels in today's world whereby the Bible is misused to control and extort people is a scary reality we face and can be used to keep many people down, in the dirt unable to strive through their struggles and traumas.

We still see fellow citizens in Africa using the Bible to extort other human beings. I am from African heritage and was born in Nigeria, where people's wages are very small, yet they donate enough money to the churches whose pastors own their own private jets! Who is fooling whom? Could the tithes donated to the pastors be the proceeds of crime? There are many disturbing stories around the world, and I feel that if there is no unity in Africa, the centre of the world, and if there is no mutual respect between races, then how can there be love? Xenophobia, tribalism, and cannibalism are dividing Africans, and the stigma of slavery still lives with us.

---

[1] In the business of enslavement the British Royal family had instructed Sir John Hawkins (slave master and British naval commander) to not take people from Africa against their wishes and to not be forceful with his slavery business at the time. Hawkins used different tactics to achieve his goal of enslavement, luring people aboard boats with the promise of a better life in the western world.

One of the positive outcomes I'm hoping for is to create awareness about innocent people dying behind the scenes, and I use Alex's experience to inspire people who could be suffering from post-traumatic stress disorder (PTSD). No matter which situation you find yourself in, you can defeat PTSD. Follow this story with full attention, and you will understand how he lived with trauma and refused to be defeated by it. We need to educate ignoramuses about leaving the past in the past, and we must remind Africans to unite, let God be the judge, and allow love to flow.

Post-Traumatic Stress Disorder (PTSD)

Trauma is referred to as any event or experience that changes your vision of yourself and of the world. When brain activity is altered by traumatic events, it can be a heavy burden to carry because the brain always finds it difficult to process extraordinary circumstances. Heavy burdens like PTSD could then put you in a situation where you battle with your mind every day, and by all means it's a battle you have to continue to win. PTSD does have a negative effect on your mental and physical health. The mental health effect should not be taken for granted because the end result could be disastrous. I come from the part of the world where our perception of madness is a naked man walking the street and talking to himself. The dangerous ones are the trendy-looking schizophrenics because they can do the unthinkable at any time. Most of us, at some point in our lives, have had some unresolved occurrences that might leave some PTSD demons in us. Such demons could be severe anxiety, hypervigilance, psychogenic flashbacks, uncontrollable thoughts, nightmares, pseudo hallucinations, explosive anger and more. PTSD puts one in a vulnerable place mentally and that vulnerability can be dangerous to oneself and society.

Alex was ordered by the court to get compulsory anger management before the penny dropped about his PTSD. He has since gone for many sessions and done rigorous research about PTSD. I was flabbergasted when he told me most of his troubles were traced back to past occurrences. Anything unresolved within our energy field will keep manifesting itself in our mental and physical lives. I am even starting to think that his situation might be hyperarousal because of the height of his anxiety. He's overly sensitive and responsive to stimuli and the events around him; it was a difficult task to get him to sit still and get his full account to prepare this book. As much as you try to stay out of trouble, there are many negativities around the world that can trigger the demon in you, which then makes you feel violated or disrespected, especially when you have a bad temper. The person could be completely out of order, but the condition would make you throw a mini tantrum. The aggression in your response would always make you come across as the guilty one; at this time, people may forget the real cause of the fight, and you will be judged based on the extent you have gone to defend your own honour. You always get victimised as a result. I relate with Alex on many levels; it's one of the reasons I'm so fascinated about his story.

After Alex was ordered by court to get compulsory anger management, he was placed under three months' house arrest with an electronic tag. When he told me about the fact that his long-term girlfriend gave false witness against him in court, I was shocked. Why would someone go to such extent to ruin another person's life? I would like to think Alex was victimised. You can agree with me that a woman you have dated for five years knows your weaknesses and strengths! Such was the case with the applicant of the aforementioned case. She knew the kind of record Alex had with the cops, and she used it to exaggerate the confrontation that went down between them. She lied that Alex hit her, but he never laid a finger on her. The judicial system in most Western countries makes one's criminal record so powerful that one can be innocent and still get indicted for a crime one never committed. I would have thought the best and fairest way to get an unbiased decision in court would be that a bad record does not make you guilty, and a good record does not make you innocent. Alex was victimised by the institution, and he was victimised by someone he held close.

Hopefully, Alex's testimony through this book will help people understand the danger that PTSD poses. The emotional and physical effects of PTSD have a connection in the traumatic event because people respond physiologically as their sympathetic nervous systems trigger the response to fracas. Personally, I think many people around the world may be suffering from some form of PTSD, although undiagnosed. There are so many unrests and tensions globally that mentally weak people are unable to process. The daunting horrors of slavery and the stigma, also the present institutional racism have damaged people's perception of things. Although it was claimed to be long gone with a phoney equality campaign, it has advanced and operated in a subtle way. It is operated through governmental institutions and is backed up with unjust policies. This makes the government set up Ponzi schemes to unsettle ethnic minorities, and they do not mind punishing some of their own race as long as they are low-class citizens. This does put affected people in mental bondage, and mental bondage is invisible violence! It makes the victims self-contained, which would make it impossible to challenge the beliefs of thoughts that control him.

Borderline Personality Disorder (BPD)

Borderline personality disorder, otherwise known as emotional dysregulation disorder, is a mental disorder characterised by mood swings in behaviour and relationship. BDP is a very complicated mental case, and more people should be aware of it. I feel many people are living with this mental situation without realising it, based on symptoms collected during my research on this topic. According to the National Health Service in the UK; The symptoms include fear of abandonment, unstable relationships, unstable self-image, impulsive risky behaviours, self-harm and suicide, intense mood swings, chronic feelings of emptiness, explosive anger, paranoia, and dissociation.[2] As you read, you will understand why I have chosen to talk about BPD. Although Alex may not have been diagnosed with BPD, his behaviour in the past displays 70 per cent of BPD's symptoms. People with BDP have a fear of being abandoned even though it could be an imaginary threat, and tend to take drastic measures in their quest to avoid being left

---

[2] For more information refer to https://www.nhs.uk/Conditions/borderline-personality-disorder/

alone. They can go as far as being clingy and jealous, and they go on to track loved ones' movements. They may even physically block loved ones from walking out on them. They almost always end up getting abandoned.

These traits make the relationship unstable and make it difficult to maintain healthy relationships. They make the person suffering from it super needy, mistrusting, and overly passionate. According to the National Institute of Mental Health, a person with BDP tends to have a very black and white way of thinking about people, seeing them as all good or all bad. This causes frequently shifting attitudes towards others that range from extreme closeness to extreme dislike or anger.[3] Alex's shambolic relationships and the decisions he made that did not go well for him show that these complications could be due to BPD. His constant shifting of ideas, what he wanted in life, and the people he wanted to be associated with also indicate signs of BPD. He also has eccentric and impulsive behaviours that are associated with BPD. These behaviours are said to put individuals in danger, such as binge eating, drug abuse,

---

[3] For more information refer to https://www.nimh.nih.gov/health/topics/borderline-personality-disorder/index.shtml

reckless driving, alcohol abuse, or unsafe sex. Clearly, engaging in these activities makes them feel better temporarily, but they can do more harm than good in the long run to themselves and their close relationships.

Research showed about 10 per cent of people with BPD take their own lives. Although in most cases self-harming behaviours are non-suicidal, it is essential that we collectively raise awareness about this mental condition to save people around the world and set free such troubled minds. Emotional vulnerability is common in society today; one sees people swing from extreme happiness to despair frequently, and such mood swings are often triggered by minor things that most people may not pay attention to, such as people being too preoccupied to say hello. Yes, such moods tend to pass quickly, but they are another symptom of BPD.

Anger Management

Explosive anger, which is often triggered, is another symptom. This book will show how temperamental Alex is based on some exaggerated or disproportional reaction to situations that could be handled differently. Alex is very regretful about some of these actions, but he affirmed they were done through provocation. Research showed most of these angers are noticeable when they are directed outwardly toward others and happen as a result of a genuine trigger. Amongst many other BPD symptoms is a chronic feeling of emptiness, where people feel there is something missing in them, some hole or emptiness. Such people may feel they are less important, and they desperately try to fill the void with negative things like sex, food, drugs, or validation from people around them and on social media.

Anxiety

Anxiety is a normal reaction to stress and one can benefit from it sometimes because it helps us to prepare for danger and concentrate. America Psychiatric Association (APA) affirmed; Anxiety disorders differ from normal feelings of nervousness and anxiousness, and involve excessive fear of anxiety. Anxiety disorders are the most common of mental disorders and affect nearly 30% of adults at some point of their lives. Even though anxiety disorders has no permanent cure, but they are treatable and can help people lead normal meaningful lives.

We have situations like Generalized Anxiety Disorder (GAD), It is defined as an uncontrollable disposition to worry about one's welfare and that of one's immediate kin. Associated manifestations include arousal, vigilance, vigilance, tension, irritability, unrestful sleep, and gastrointestinal distress.[4]

---

[4] HS Akiskal, Acta Psychiatrica Scandinavica 98, 66-73, 1998

Sex Addiction

Sexual addiction is a condition in which an individual cannot manage their sexual behaviour. Persistent sexual thoughts affect their ability to work, maintain relationships, and fulfil their daily activities.[5]

This behaviour disorder is known as Satyriasis in males and nymphomania in females. Sexual dependency, hypersexuality, and compulsive sexual behaviour.

"Sexual addiction, also often referred to as hypersexuality, sexual dependency and compulsive sexual behaviour disorder, is a condition that involves the sufferer becoming excessively preoccupied with thoughts or behaviours that give a desired sexual effect. Hypersexuality, sexual dependency and compulsive sexual behaviour disorder are other name for sexual addiction. As with other dependencies, sexual addiction is a condition that involves the sufferer becoming excessively

[5] Christian Nordqvist, Medical News Today, updated 20 Dec 2017

preoccupied with thoughts or behaviours that give a desired effect. It involves spending an exorbitant amount of time thinking about and/or engaging in sexually addictive behaviours."[6]

[6] Dryden-Edwards, R. (eds.) 2018. Sexual Addiction Assessment Treatment & Recovery – MedicineNet.

Xenophobia

Xenophobia is originated from Greek words, Xenos in Greek means 'the stranger and the guest and phobos means 'fear'. Xenophobia is understood as the 'fear of stranger' but typically, it is understood to mean the 'hatred of strangers'.[7] It can be defined as, "an attitudinal orientation of hostility against non-natives in a given populations".[8]

---

[7] Smelser, N. J. and Baltes, P.B. (eds.) 2001. International Encyclopaedia of the Social and Behavioural Sciences. Elsevier. Oxford Science Ltd.

[8] Boehnke, Klaude in NGO Working Group on Migration and Xenophobia for the World Conference (In International Migration, Racism, Discrimination and Xenophobia, 2001. A publication jointly produced by ILO, IOM, OHCHR, in consultation with UNHCR. Page 2.

There is difference between xenophobia and racism, xenophobia is said to imply behaviour based on the idea that the other is foreign to or originates from outside the community or nation, while racism usually entails distinction based on physical characteristic differences, such as skin colour, hair type, facial features.[9]

[9] (NGO Working Group on Migration and Xenephobia for the World Conference (in International Migration, Racism, Discrimination and Xenephobia, 2001. A publication jointly produced by ILO, IOM, OHCHR, in consultation with UNHCR)

Young and Innocent

Alex emphasised his belief in God and was confident about God's presence in his life from a very young age. According to him, his father was a politician and a big shot in his country of origin. He described his father as a distinguished gentleman and a no-nonsense disciplinarian who had passion for his job. He described his father as his hero and affirmed he was a worthy hero because of his father's philosophy of life. He maintained, "I see my father as my hero because of his unique way of bringing up his kids without over pampering any of us. He had a rough journey to the top of his game. However, he defied the odds by achieving his goals while he was living. He came from a small village, where most of the indigenes were known for farming, and he was still able to serve his country as a military man before going on to studying political science at university."

When talking about his mum, Alex says "it is often said that a good and strong woman is the strength of her husband,

and this is the easiest way to describe my unbiased mum. She was a selfless and prayerful lady who stood right next to her husband from the moment she laid eyes on him to the very end when he passed on. They met when my father was in the military and struggling hard, but she chose not to be swayed by richly things of the world. She invested her life with dedication to her family. She does not care about savings because she has always emphasised that she's gotten what she wanted in the family God gave her."

Alex went further to praise his mum. "She enjoyed her life with full respect from her family, and as a widow, she still benefits from the legacy her heartthrob left behind, including how my egghead siblings and I stay determined to not let our father's legacy die. I see her as a mother of the world because she never discriminates against anyone, and she opens the doors of her house for all to come in. She is the only person who can yell at me without me saying a word, because whatever she might be complaining about would be out of love. I love you, Mother, and it is you and I in the next world. Despite how difficult my parents' relationship was sometimes, Mother never budged.

"It was a kind of an old-fashioned love, where her husband could not do anything wrong. I was raised with love; it was a bit of tough love sometimes, but it was exactly what a curious and stubborn kid like me needed." Alex talked in great depth about his family and how his father joined the military as a teenager before dropping the military force to start a new career in politics. He became a fearless politician who stood by what he believed until the day he died. Alex affirmed, "He was not scared to punish my siblings and me when we misbehaved. Frog jumps[10] were his favourite kind of punishment. People can claim that it's a form of exercise, but I can tell you we did not see it that way. We saw it as a blatant punishment. I never liked it at the time, but when I think about it as an adult, I'm glad it happened because it gave me the mental ability to withstand the testing periods in life. Although he was a very strict man, he loved his family and made sure he protected us to the end. He even protected us when he was close to

[10] A frog jump involves holding your ears, squatting and jumping to move forward

his death. He knew he was going but never told any of us about his terminal illness. I try to imagine the kind of agony he must have been going through, knowing that it was just a matter of time before he was mourned."

Alex was regretful for causing his parents different problems, but he was still very thankful to survive some self-inflicted pain because he sees it as an opportunity to raise awareness about the danger surrounding teenagers in the habit of running away from home at an early age. He added, "I caused my dad a lot of problems as a teenager. Some problems were beyond my control, and some were a result of stupidity. If I could turn back the hands of time, I would have done things differently. I guess I thought he was going to be around for a very long time and I took his love for granted. I didn't know I was hurting him or my mum; I was simply confused and wanted to see what this world was all about."

His traumatic encounter started at the age of five when he was run over by a car and was unconscious for almost a week. His exact comment about the accident was, "Luckily I survived the ordeal. Even though I survived, it causes me problems today. I get psychogenic flashbacks about the accident when crossing the road, but I guess it is a price I have to pay for cheating death." He thought because he survived the accident, it was the end of that situation, but he was met with constant unpleasant flashbacks decades afterwards. This is why I personally think more awareness should be raised about PTSD to enable people get the right help when Mother Nature gives us more than we bargain for in life.

As a teenager, Alex tried to find himself and started rebelling. He was always on the run, trying to live a rule-less life away from his parents, who he felt were too strict at the time. He told me his absconding habit started when he met his then best friend, John. John lived in a bigger city with more activities and attractions, and it didn't take John long to convince Alex to come to the bigger city with him. He started running away from home when he met John, who told him about life in the big city with his family. He met him at private school, where his parents sent him to so he could have a solid education. Although he regret causing his parents problem, but does not regret his early exposure to the street. It was dangerous at the time, but the big guy upstairs had his back and saw him through what could have taken his life. His experiences at that time are part of the tools he use to get on with life today. He ran away from home and followed John to the big city.

He loved city life and visited it over and over. The first few times he travelled, his parents were in distress, praying he would not get himself in trouble or get himself killed. He felt he has special protection from God and it's the reason he's still alive today. He was young and stupid, and he never stopped gallivanting, but God preserved his life so he could share this testimony. He said the first time he realised his case with God was different was when he escaped an accident that took the lives of all the passengers on a bus. Bus drivers at the motor park had to queue up and wait for their turn to load before going on a three-and-a-half-hour journey from his home to the bigger city. He was on a bus that was fully loaded, ready to go before he told the driver he had forgotten something because his mind was telling him to get off the bus. He knew that he would have to wait longer for the next bus to load, but the vibrations in his body would not let him go with that bus. He waited over an hour to finally embark on the journey. They travelled for two hours, and then they saw the bus in a ditch following a serious accident. Everybody on the bus had died on the spot. He started shaking and could not talk. He was branded special in God's eyes by his family when he told them about his miraculous escape from the accident.

Alex attended Fela Kuti's shrine every Friday while he was in Lagos, even though it was very rare to see teenagers in such an environment. He said he'd been around older people drinking and smoking, but it never made him grow up too quick mentally. As a Nigerian myself, I can confirm the government saw Fela Kuti as a threat because he was an activist who expressed himself through his songs. People loved him because he was not afraid to have a dig at the government, but the environment was always dangerous because he was target of the military government at the time Alex attended.

"We had military leaders at the time I started going to see Fela on stage. He and his audience were targets for military harassment. They chased us down the streets, shooting at us. Sometimes we had to do zigzag running to escape the bullets. This never stopped me from attending, so you can see that I lived my teenage life dangerously. My living arrangements then were rough because I ran away from home and was not yet sixteen years old. I stayed at John's house until his dad saw me in the house and chased me back home. I left their house but slept in unoccupied buildings. On one occasion, I was sleeping and was discovered by security guards during the night. I tried to explain myself but was met with repeated slaps. They blew their whistles and woke the people in the neighbourhood, telling them that they had found a thief. People were so barbaric that they did not ask what I had stolen. I was attacked and battered with sticks and stones. I thought that was the end of me because I was aware of the jungle justice in Nigeria. When they caught petty thieves, they killed them on the spot. Although I survived it, the ordeal made me realise that many innocent people would have died as a result of barbarism. My head was swollen, and I was crying and bleeding everywhere. I kept screaming that I had run away from home and was not trying to steal from anyone. One of the people told them to hear me out, and I was given the benefit of the doubt."

Out of panic, Alex travelled back home the next day, still in shock about the misunderstanding that could have taken his life. He summoned the courage to share the experience with his mum, and she cried, asking him what she has done for Alex to keep living his life in danger. He felt sorry about how emotional his mum was and tried to stay focused, but that never lasted long. Soon he'd get into more mischief.

With persistent effort from his parents not giving up on him and trying everything so he could make something out of his life, he gained admission into a higher institution and was handed an opportunity to change his life around. It did not last long because Alex joined a secret confraternity on campus. This involved people fighting and killing each other. Although he maintained he never got involved in taking anybody's life, he got into few fights, and he says he is lucky to be alive today.

"My family warned me against gangs like this before I went to university. I was so sure that I would make my family proud by not joining this gang. I tried my very best to avoid these people—until I saw this nice young man who was very attentive and showed me around the campus. It did not at all come into my mind that he could be one of them; I was under the impression that you could always tell from afar what the members of this dangerous confraternity looked like. He was very kind to me, and I was so confident that I had a friend in him. What made the matter worse was that my dad came to campus to see me with his police escort. This guy saw my dad and asked me more about my family. I told him who my dad was. I did not know that they were looking for people from solid backgrounds."

Alex was later invited to attend a party, not knowing that his initiation was about to take place. On getting to this party venue, the friend that took him disappeared into the crowd, where everybody was wearing black. There were no girls. That was the moment the penny dropped. He knew he was about to join the forbidden gang, but it was a little too late because there was no hiding place for him anymore. He gave in and joined the gang. At this stage, he told himself that the only thing he could do was keep himself safe and stay alive. They were always told in advance when a fight was coming up, and he was always observant. He made sure he was not available before any fight started. He always travelled to hang out with his friends in Lagos, and he would find a way to send a message to his family that he was safe before they saw any fights on the television because they were always on the news.

He claimed to use that opportunity of his brotherhood confraternity to call his bullies to order because it was always easier to deal with civilians at the time. When you carry the tag of secret cult, nobody wants to disrespect you because they can't predict what your reaction will be. He got the best girls at the time because young women always felt they needed protection. "It got to a point where I started liking older women; it became a fantasy in my head that I was curious to explore. In case you want to know if I ever fulfilled that fantasy, I did! I became an idol in my house. My parents and siblings let me have my way because they were unsure what stunt I would pull next. My perseverance was noticed by people around me at the time. This includes those who knew me personally and those who knew about me."

One of the reasons I thought Alex had messed up experiences as a youth is his story with a local booze seller when he was growing up. What teenager craves an unusual fantasy of having coitus with someone old enough to be his mum? However, it makes more sense to me when therapy linked Alex's sexcapade with his sexual abuse at the tender age of nine. We live in a messed-up world where a woman in her thirties felt it was acceptable to have sex with nine-year-old Alex. What I found really brave about Alex is that despite the link with his ordeals, he still accepts responsibility for his silliness, which was put down to his PTSD. I was curious to know the story of the booze seller, and I asked him to elaborate how it all happened.

He told me he attended the woman's shop every day to drink with his entourage. He later told one of his squad about his desire to have coitus with this woman; he said it seemed impossible, but he was thinking out loud in front of his friends. One of his friends by the name of Pius encouraged him to go for it, but still he could not summon the courage. Pius later decided to approach this woman and let her know what Alex's desire was. He was gobsmacked because this woman gave in to his desire to be intimate with her, but she warned him not to mess about or he would find out what she was made of. He thought it was just a cheap bluff, but he was wrong. The panic was triggered when the woman in question appeared in Alex's dream, trying to attack him.

"To rewind the story a little, she told me to meet her in a hotel uptown. I met up with her for a couple of hours, and we had coitus. She immediately asked me for money because she noticed I had my own car, even as a teenager. She didn't know that my mum had given it to me when my dad had bought her a new car. I didn't have the money she asked me for, and I decided to start avoiding her. One day I was sleeping, and this woman appeared in my dream, ordering me to follow her. I rebuked her in God's name. I woke up and could not move my body. At this time, I started to pray, and I felt better and went back to sleep. She reappeared in my dream, still telling me I had to follow her!

At this time, I jumped up, ran to my mum's room, and knocked emphatically! My mum opened the door and asked me what the matter was. I told her there was a particular woman who kept appearing in my dream, telling me to follow her. The first question my mum asked me was if I had had sex with the woman, and I didn't have any choice but to confirm that I had. She held my hands and prayed for hours. From that moment, the woman never appeared in my dreams again, and she always looked away when she saw me on the street. In that moment, I believed that there were evil spirits, and I experienced supernatural powers of Almighty God."

Alex told his friends what he had encountered, and everybody was surprised about what had happened. They even found Alex's confession to his mum super funny. Alex decided to drop out of university not long after what he referred to as "the demonic encounter with the booze seller." He said it was too dangerous for him to go back to university. His focus shifted to travelling out of the country, to a Western country. Although his dad was completely against the idea, Alex was stubborn, and when he set his mind on something, it was impossible to stop him. He travelled back and forth to Lagos, carrying out research about travelling to America, because that had always been the country in which he wanted to live. He had relatives and family friends living in America, and they had told him many fantastic stories about the country. His dad was strongly against it and was bringing the roof down about Alex dropping out from university. He wanted to arrange for Alex to go to a different university.

"I had to listen to him at some point because I didn't have any money of my own. I got admission into a different university, and I was incognito because I didn't want people in the same confraternity knowing my identity; the brotherhood and secret cults were all over universities in Nigeria. I didn't want problems or stress, and so I wanted to stay unknown. It didn't work for long—I was found out. I had to do the inevitable and drop out of university again. I couldn't tell my family what the problem was, and it became such a serious problem that my dad did not talk to me for a while. I decided to find my own way by stealing from my dad to embark on a road journey through Africa and find my way to Europe. I got stranded in the Ivory Coast, a francophone country, even though I could not speak French."

The Prodigal Son

What teenager leaves his country with a world map in his hand, relying totally on strangers to survive? Some people would say a stupid little boy, and some would say an adventurous young man. Whatever your perspective might be, it was the case with Alex Benjamin. It was very shallow of him, but he was too stubborn to change his mind from the moment he made the decision. It took him a whole day to arrive at the Ivory Coast because he travelled by road. He had to find his way and change from one public transportation to another. The Ivory Coast was not meant to be his final destination, but he was robbed and extorted by men in uniform between Ghana and the Ivory Coast border. He had to come to terms that the Ivory Coast would be his home for a long time. He gallivanted for hours in the country, trying to figure out what approach he needed to take in order to think of a permanent solution.

He kept walking around the country with his life flooding out of his eyes. The moment he realised he had made the mistake of his life by embarking on that journey, he could not control his tears because of the seriousness of the situation. He knew if he didn't make the right move, it would cost him his life—and nobody understood a word he was saying. Everybody was speaking French, and he said to himself that he was doomed. The only cash he had left on him was 5CFA[11], which was just enough for him to buy one meal! However, he decided to use that money for a haircut rather than a meal. Of course he was hungry, but the only thing he had left was his instinct and God leading him. His mind kept saying to him to have a haircut. He obeyed his instinct and looked for barbershop.

After a short period of time, he found a barbershop. He went to the shop gesticulating; there was no other way to communicate. The barber decided to try English with him, and it worked because Nigeria's official language is English. He screamed for enjoy as he saw someone with whom to share his ordeal. He was very friendly and told him about what Alex was getting myself into. He said that he and four others slept in the shop. Alex asked where the others were,

[11] CFA – Currency of the African Financial Community

and he replied that they had gone to the seaport to hustle, hoping there might be opportunity for them to stowaway or get a cabin connection. A stowaway is a person who hides in a ship, and a cabin connection is with the captain's consent. Cabin connection was always super expensive because you have a 95 per cent chance of getting there alive. This was not the case with stowaways, because if you get caught hiding, there is always a possibility that you will be thrown into the sea because it is the easiest way for the captain of the ship to avoid being fined. Alex was told many of their friends from the barbershop hid in ships, but they didn't hear back from them. Even so, many people who were aware of this risk were still willing to go ahead.

"It was not long before it started to get dark. He asked me where I planned on sleeping. I thought it would be a fantastic idea to negotiate for a corner in the barber's shop, and I refused to leave the shop. I knew my only chance of security that night was to sleep in the shop because they were fellow Nigerians trying to find a way out, and it was in the interest of togetherness on the street for real to recognise real!"

Alex was later kicked out of the barbershop because the decision was not the barber's alone to make. Alex decided to not leave the area in case the barber took pity on him later. At two in the morning, in the middle of the night, he was lying on the bench outside and panicking. Then he saw a taxi pull over and the other boys arrived back from the seaports. When the barber heard their voices, he opened the door, and Alex started begging all of them to let him stay. They had a five-minute meeting inside, and they agreed for him to stay until daybreak. He woke up before everybody and started to clean everywhere. By the time they got up, he told them to step out so he could sweep the shop. When he finished cleaning, they reconsidered and told him to stay for the time being on the condition that he would clean on a regular basis. At this point, Alex started to feed on their leftovers. Anytime they felt he had done something wrong, they threw their leftovers in the bin.

Two weeks passed, and Alex was still in search of a job to be able to stand on his own two feet. He finally got a job at the airport, helping people to carry their baggage. It was a very low income, and what he was paid daily only bought him something to eat. He had to walk five miles to and from work every day. He was constantly harassed by the Ivoirians to go back to his country. He did not like the discrimination, but there was nothing he could do about it. He hadn't heard of the words *xenophobia* or *racism* at the time. "I was brought up with love, and I never thought there could be any form of hatred from anybody, especially not your fellow African people. I kept my head down and went about my business.

"It did not take long before I was kicked out of the barbershop, and I went to sleep by the beachside. I slept near the beach for three days before I was caught by the people in the neighbourhood. I was beaten blue and black, and they kept shouting at me that I should go back to my country. After twenty minutes of being attacked, I staggered away, but at this moment they searched for a tyre and put it around my neck. They were ready to set me ablaze. I had a small New Testament Bible in my pocket, and I brought it out, pleading with them for mercy. God again intervened and spoke through one of the leader's heart. He ordered them to let me go, and surprisingly I was allowed to walk."

This part of Alex's story brought tears to my eyes because I could not comprehend how people could act with total disrespect for humanity. I felt it was cowardly, and I sincerely sympathised with black heritage and their level of ignorance. Dislike and prejudice against people from other countries is not going to make one's life or country better! It only separates us and deprives us of finding our true identities. Alex told me the people were ready to kill him, and some were disappointed they'd let him go.

He had to look around for a better place to stay the next day. He saw this partially built building and spoke with the owner of the property to ask if he would allow him to sleep there for some time until he was able to find his way. He agreed on the condition that Alex did hard labour for him by using his head to lift building blocks every day—and he still had to do his airport job because both payments were unbelievably small.

"Thank God that I didn't give up my airport job because it was not long before I saw a lady at the airport who came from the same city as me in Nigeria. She asked what I was doing there and said I was too young to be in that country myself. She asked who my parents were and where they were. I told her, and something unexpected happened. She knew my parents, and she didn't believe a son of a reputable politician would be helping people carry baggage in a different country. She told me she knew my family, and we shared pleasantries. I thought it was the end of it until I saw this woman few weeks later. She had gone to my house in Nigeria to confirm they were looking for any of their kids. My family thought I was dead and was ecstatic about the news the lady brought. She later came with letters from every member of my family, and my dad's letter was the most anticipated one because I didn't know what his reaction was going to be.

I jumped for joy when I opened my dad's letter. He wrote in it that I was forgiven, and he took my case to be like the prodigal son in the Bible. I should come home like a beggar in a song. He said that if I had used the money I'd stolen to enjoy myself, he would be upset, but he said that he was proud of me for trying to find my own way in life. They sent me money for transportation. This was big money that I didn't think I would get for a decade. I later travelled back to Nigeria, and it was a joyful day when I was reunited with my family. Mother wept uncontrollably, but it was happy tears because they thought they had lost me. I apologised to everybody, my mother in particular, for the trouble I had put them through when I disappeared."

If we look around us today, there are extraordinary circumstances around the world like; 21st slavery in Libya. In case people are still wondering how victims of Libya slavery came about, they need not look or think further because this are the unlucky people that went on similar journey to Alex Benjamin's journey. Alex was lucky to return home safely, but I think more awareness need to be raised for people that travel illegally by road in Africa. There is no account for such people lives and majority always end up dead or captured. It is so embarrassing and disgraceful that all these major news platforms don't say anything about this catastrophic twenty first century slavery going on in Libya. This institutional racism and selfish interests can tear us all apart. Something has to be done about this because it's utterly disgusting to see such cruelty to humanity in this day and age. The oppressors need to leave the oppressed be for love and peace to reign all over the world.

Welcome to America

It was a new dawn for Alex after reuniting with his family. He changed his ways to make up for the time spent apart from his family. He took it upon himself to ask permission for anything he needed to do. Believe it or not, Alex was a changed man, and he had learnt serious lesson about life. He was attentive, submissive, and religious. "Mother gave me close marking and took me with her to the business she owned in town. I followed her to prayer meetings, Bible studies, and night vigils, on top of the compulsory Sunday service. It was a routine that went on for a very long time, and it did not take long before I became dedicated to praying and fasting.

"It was at this moment that I presented my case before the supremo of heaven and earth regarding my desire to travel to America and make a fresh start with my life. I didn't have any idea of what to do, and I placed all my trust and belief in God. Some non-believers might argue that it was a stupid thing to do, but that was all I knew at the time. I had to trust my belief and let awesome God take control. I started street evangelism, preaching about the splendour of Almighty God. People thought I was mad because I was the last person they were expecting to see ringing a bell up and down and preaching the good news.

"One Sunday after service, the pastor called my name in front of the congregation and asked me to stay behind. I did as I was told, and the pastor told me to read the book of Psalms from beginning to end. I did as I was told, and the pastor prayed for protection on me and for a new door to be opened for me, as he was shown in his vision."

Alex has always been blessed with the gift of dream. He sees what is going to happen in his dream before watching it manifest. He told his pastor about this gift and shared with him every relevant dream he had experienced. When there was any sign of a problem, he dealt with it, together with his pastor, by fasting and praying. He told me how God ordered him in his dream to preach the good word use his life as an example of greatness. It could be seen as superstitious, but I believe it because I have similar gift.

He told his pastor about this, and the pastor told him that God wanted him to be a minister for him. He was confused because one of his few fears in life was facing a crowd to speak. "I have a weird personality, and I don't like people seeing my shyness. People could argue that, because when I get used to people around me, I can suddenly become an extrovert. The pastor took me with him to his prayer meetings, and I could tell God was happy with me because the visions in my dreams became clearer. It was during this period that I dreamt about travelling to America. I told my pastor about what I saw in my dream, and he said that if I had my own ideas about how to embark on the journey, then I should go for it. He said the Lord had spoken. Normally, people go to the high commission of the country they intend to travel to obtain a visa to allow them to go on the journey. In my case, I was young, and my dad was not buying it. From the little you know about me, I am sure you can guess what step I took next. It was registered in my heart, and no one was going to stop me from making my own move. I took it easy, trying not to take any drastic measure like I had with my shambolic Ivory Coast tour.

"Around this time, I was buying and selling fairly used clothes to my friends. My mum gave me money to do that just to keep me busy so I would not get up to any mischief. I had my spot where I bought outfits and designer brands; I focused on this business to fight the demon in me because my instinct kept pushing me to go for it. I did not want to let my family down for a second time, but a curious boy wants what he wants. I normally bought used clothes from Lagos, where my then best friend John lived. I travelled down to Lagos and went straight to do my shopping so I could resell to make a profit. However, there was no way I could go to Lagos without going to my best friend's house to see him. I got there, and we exchanged pleasantries because we were ecstatic to see each other. He checked the clothes I had purchased for resale. He picked one pair of immaculate white Levi skinny jeans and asked if he could borrow them from me because he wanted to drive his auntie to the airport. His auntie was based in America, and I'd seen her at my friend's house. I did not hesitate to lend him the jeans because he promised to give them back to me in couple of hours, after he had come back. Borrowing clothes from each other was a normal thing at the time. To cut a long story short, I waited for my friend for two hours before his little brother, now a blessed memory, came to tell me my friend was on his way to the United States. I was shocked. I felt disappointed that he didn't have the decency to tell me he was leaving the country. I travelled back home, heartbroken that I would not see him for a while and that he felt the need to keep it a secret."

When Alex got back home, his behaviour changed. He didn't bother to sell anything he'd bought, and the urgency to travel intensified. He went to his pastor and told him he was ready to go on a journey to America. The pastor told Alex God had spoken, and he should go for it. This time, he chose to carry his parents along. He woke both of them up in the middle of the night to tell them he was ready to embark on his long anticipated journey to the United States.

His dad asked him why he didn't wait for day to break before having the conversation with them. He answered, "Based on the seriousness of the conversation, I prefer to discuss it at this time." He told them he was ready to go, and he told his father he needed some money. His father agreed to give him some money on one condition: if he wasted the money, he was not to come back to the house again. He paused and thought about it for few minutes. He knew how principled his dad was, and he could tell he was serious about him not coming back to the house if he squandered the money. However, he agreed to the condition, and the money was arranged for him.

Alex mum followed him to where he would get public transport on the day he was leaving. She prayed for him and hugged him goodbye. The airport he was supposed to travel from was Lagos, and so he travelled there. When he got to Lagos, he went to some location called Oluwole, where you could get any passport you want. He got himself a foreign passport and kept it where he was staying temporarily in Lagos. He later went to the airport to find the top immigration officer, who would take payment and put him on the plane without overly checking his passport because it wasn't his picture on the passport page. It looked like him a little. Alex plan worked. He found himself a top Nigerian immigration officer who was willing to compromise his ethics by accepting his payment. He put him on a flight within no time. They had a stopover and he passed through their immigration with ease. They looked at his passport, passed it back to him, and wished him a safe journey. He had passed his first test, but the bigger—or biggest—test was still coming, the final destination America.

He got to the airport and gave himself up by telling them was he holding a passport that did not belong to him. They were shocked by the confession and took him to a room. They pampered him with food and hot beverages while he waited to be interrogated. He told the truth, and they locked him up for few days. While he was locked up, he started to fast and pray. He told people he met while locked up about God and how he would receive favour in the hands of immigration. He met different ethnicities there, and they laughed at him, saying; How would they let him go if he had a passport that did not belong to him? He never panicked because he was confident that God was trying to show him it was his doing. He slept on the fourth day, and God came to him in his dream again. He told him he was going to be released the next day, and he woke up joyful.

Believe it or not, Alex was allowed to enter the United States the next day. He showed me the temporary admission paperwork that was given to him, and he was told to report back three months later. He started a new life in America, he was later granted green card and has lived in the United States for over two decades.

The Waiting Game

"I had already started a new life in America. It was a period in my life where all my traumatic experiences had dented my reasoning and perception. I wanted a stage to play for a long time, and I finally found one, but I was unable to play. I became too anxious, and anxiety is something that has to be dealt with because it can kill. People can have heart attacks or strokes for being too anxious about what is to come. It is a bad thing to live in the past because it is a sign of depression, but it can be worse to live in the future because it is sign of anxiety. It didn't take long before I started to prioritise partying over improving my life. The wrong decisions I made at the time taught me that people will criticize you no matter how bad or good you are, and so you have to make sure you do not let outer noise disturb your inner voice. Not everybody you take advice from has the knowledge to give sound advice. Misleading you is easy when you run to every Tom, Dick, and Harry for advice. I made up my mind that every negative or compromised situation I found myself in must be taken as a learning curve, and I had to keep on moving. I later gave myself a reality check and decided to go back to college. It was not a course I wanted to do, but I had to get myself on the academic platform. I would let down myself and the family if I was to do otherwise. I did a three-month short course to find a way to do the law course I have always wanted to do. I finished that course and started to work long shifts because bills needed to be paid."

It did not take long before Alex bumped into John, his childhood best friend who'd left without saying goodbye to him. John apologised and told him he didn't have no choice and it was his belief that if he told people what he was getting up to, it would not happen. They became best buddies again and lived together until things got better for them and they were able to get proper accommodations. It was a difficult task for Alex and John to live together because John was living with his partner, but Alex had to endure the temporary arrangement because of his financial status at the time. Responsibilities increased for Alex and more money was needed.

"The wait for something great to happen, or for the big break to manifest, was something I did not handle particularly well, but I found my way around it. I managed to not get involved in anything like class A drugs because it only gives a temporary comfort but does not solve the actual problem. I smoked a bit of cannabis just for fun, but I always made sure I was not depending on it to ease whatever stress I was going through. I kept trying everything and studying everything so that I could power my way to the top. It was at this stage that I realised that even though America is a country where different ethnic backgrounds lives, the ethnic minorities struggle ten times more than white Americans. I am not trying to raise unnecessary controversy, but based on my experience, the stigma of being black still subconsciously has an effect on how you are going to be perceived and treated. My highest qualification is a master's degree. I have done countless training courses, seminars, weekend workshops but still I could not get a job! I received different responses via e-mail, but the moment they found out about my heritage, they didn't want to know any more about me. My curriculum vitae made me qualified, but ethnicity disqualified me. Was it meant to be like that in the twenty first century? I guess not. There are different campaigns out there about equality. Are those campaigns enough? I beg to differ! I did not read anything that said that. I heard at a professional workshop that it was okay to stereotype, but you have to finesse the situation so the people in question would not know. Unfortunately, Nigeria was listed amongst the top hundred high-risk countries."

Alex feels the system has been programmed in such a way that makes it difficult for an ethnic minority to thrive. He believes they get victimised, and when they get in trouble, they put a permanent stain on their names and identities. He thinks once you get in any kind of trouble with police, there may be no second chance to get your career on track. He hopes something can be done about records held for former offenders because sometimes people with a silly criminal history need a second chance. He emphasised the biased mind-set has hindered the equality we are preaching.

Alex got himself a business start-up loan and opened a consultancy firm. It was a success, and he was able to complete his hotel project he had been trying to build for twelve years. He was thankful to God because if he had stayed defeated by inequality in society, it would have been difficult for him to move forward. "We are all waiting for that one break that changes everything. I was wise enough to join the gym and started to train away my problems.

"Growing up around love and genuine promises made me believe that life was a bed of roses where you are loved by everybody, and everything people promise you comes to pass. I never knew that life was much more difficult than that. I was branded crazy for contesting every wrong decision around me because it brings confrontation. Confrontation brings argument, argument brings hostility, and hostility brings hatred. I did not have many friends growing up; in short, John was the only friend I can think of at the time. He was the only person I felt genuine love around. Of course, I went on to have many acquaintances, but it was all about 'eat or be eaten', and no one cared about each other. I came to the conclusion that we are all alone in this life, and I don't expect anything from anybody. Not being able to trust anybody made me step up and hustle with perseverance and tenacity. I dealt with my thoughts alone by putting God first, and I hoped for the universe to favour my proactive mentality. Sometimes it did not go my way, but I knew how God operated. He felt that the answer to some of my prayers could be harmful.

"The waiting game made my anxiety worse. I took it upon myself to seek professional help from time to time so I could keep everything under control. I was given some medication to calm me down, but I refused to take it. I did not want any medication that could blow things out of proportion. I knew the easiest way to handle people's promises was to not expect anything good from anybody. I was called a pessimist, even though I've always seen myself as optimist. I had been waiting for too long, and I chose to not focus my mind on any form of promise. I managed to channel my anxiety into being more creative, and it gave me an appetite for more success."

Alex Met His Waterloo

There were lots of problems going on in Alex's relationship. His PTSD had clouded his ability to trust women. That included his then girlfriend, and it was only a matter of time before Alex separated from her. He consequently turned to a bachelor lifestyle and used endless parties to get away from the shambles in his relationship. One can learn a very big lesson from his situation because what he did was try to get away from the problem instead of facing it head-on. The comfort you get temporarily does not make the problem go away, but it might expose you to more problems through drinking and having meaningless coitus. He reunited with his best mate John, and they both partied like there was no tomorrow.

It didn't take long before there was an incident in which the police were involved, and Alex and John were co-defendants in a life-changing case. I did not get Alex's permission to write about this case. Although Alex was cleared of the case, John was indicted and was sentenced to years in prison. I asked Alex if things got back to how it had been between him and John, but Alex said they have stopped being friends since that case. He told me it was an unpleasant experience, and he felt he had to mention it to make sure people learned how to face their problems and learn from their mistakes rather than run away from them. Although Alex was cleared of the case in question, he still wasted up to five months of his life on remand while he was trying to prove his innocence.

Alex also made me realise the problem he refused to deal with has resurfaced after many years. It is impossible to maintain the same pattern and get a different result. "The world is complicated. It is important you find yourself and the right strategy that works for you to deal with future tests. As long as we are living, we always experience some testing period, and it is your responsibility to stay undefeated mentally, emotionally, and physically. I always try to advise people of all races, young and old, male and female who might have experienced some kind of traumatic experience that they get help before moving forward in life.

When you have a headache, you take paracetamol. It is the same thing in getting therapy for past traumatic experience, because PTSD is real and harmful."

A couple of weeks after Alex was cleared of the case, he started having fits from suspected epilepsy. He made it clear that no one in his family on both his mum's and dad's side had had a history of such sickness. At this point in time, I was emotional and in tears. How can one person go through everything Alex had gone through and still be laughing and moving forward in life? I wonder how he did it, but his extraordinary story is such that I felt people need to read and hear about it. I genuinely sympathise with Alex even though he still doesn't feel sorry for himself. He is still striving to improve himself and be the best version of himself.

He told me he first noticed the epilepsy attack when he slept in the bed and woke up on the floor with blood on his tongue. According to him, it happened repeatedly in his sleep, and he was not sure what it was for weeks. He tried to stay calm by not telling a soul, but on this day, Alex stayed over at a friend's house and later woke up inside an ambulance, being rushed to the hospital for urgent medical attention. He said he felt really okay and perfect. Out of curiosity, he asked the medical team what the problem was, and he was told he had suffered from a fit and passed out before his friend had dialled 911.

He was taken to the hospital for further checks before he was discharged. The doctor prescribed 500mg Tegretol tablets, one tablet to be taken three times a day, and he was told to stop drinking alcohol while they carried out further checks. He called his family in Nigeria, and they said it was not possible for him to have epilepsy; they thought it was a demonic attack because nobody in his generation had it.

Alex said "my mum started praying and sent me anointing oil from Africa to rub on my body and lick. It did not take long before it disappeared. I don't know how God did it, but I knew the big guy upstairs stepped in for me again. I was told to stop drinking, and I started smoking weed. Did God intervene through the anointing oil or the weed? I'm saying this because I ditched the Tegretol and focused on prayer, but I smoked cannabis from time to time. However he did it, I was free of epilepsy, and the fits were a thing of the past."

Shambolic Global Policies

Alex's passion about everything made me ask him about politics. I was having a normal conversation and didn't have the intention of writing about it. When we spoke and he gave his political view, I was stunned at his answers, and I felt it would be nice to let the readers know about it. He went back to his country of origin and his analysis was honest and direct.

He started by saying, "Ordinary people are being taken for fools globally! Most of the policies, rules, and regulations of countries can be questioned. I have lived in three countries since I was born. I lived in the Ivory Coast temporarily, Nigeria is my country of birth, and I have lived in America for two decades. Let me take it back to where it first started. Nigeria is a damaged country that needs divine intervention. On 1 October 1960, Nigeria was set free. The freedom has not been enjoyable for ordinary citizens of the country. I know this because I classify myself as an ordinary citizen of Nigeria. The education system is nothing to write home about, the currency is useless, the global relationship is appalling, the youth empowerment system is disgraceful, and the health system is arranged in a way that the death rate in the country can only increase over time. The democracy there has been captured by certain families so that it is starting to look like a family title. The level of nepotism in the country is worrisome. Apart from nepotism, the other thing tearing the country to pieces is bribery and corruption. My father had enemies until he entered his grave because of his principles; he was one of the few who were ready to starve rather than collect such money. He became a weird man in society because people were shocked at how anybody could be honest in Nigeria."

It was at this moment that I sat back and asked Alex's permission to add his political views in the book. He said the only logical way to move forward without any problem in Nigerian politics is to get involved in bribery and corruption or join the Ogboni fraternity. "Father was approached many times to join this ungodly secret society for power and networking. It became a standard thing, and people around the city found it difficult to believe my dad was not a member. We were always told to wait till my father died before we could be certain he had never joined the secret society. I would sometimes have doubt in my mind because people put it in my head. It was always stressful to attain some high post in Nigeria government without participating in the fraternity. Father was ready to die with a good conscience rather than join these people. It is understandable, thinking about it now, because there were loads of killings and sacrifices. I felt that was one of the main reasons my father rejected them. Many of my father's colleagues and top government officials whose families were not aware of their involvement found out when they die. It is part of their routine to remove some organs from the body whenever they pass away. Children and wives of influential deceased wait for their faith during the burial of the person in question. Oh, well. I can categorically tell the world that my father had nothing taken from his body after he passed."

Alex said he'd wished his father had taken a bribe so their family could have had more when he was a kid, but when he became a man, he felt privileged to be the seed of a man of impeccable principles. He now understands fully the message his father was trying to pass. He emphasised his father was never a greedy man; he simply wanted a high standard education for his kids and, he sought to make sure they were comfortable. "I come from a country where the leaders would steal so much money that they wouldn't be able to spend it all in their lifetimes. Instead, they bank it in the wise ones' countries. Apart from aggressive looting, there are different Ponzi schemes set up to enrich their pockets. All these lousy ideas were inherited from the wise ones—even after they claimed they had set the country free. What are you doing with people's minds after you claimed to have set them free? Different Ponzi schemes were set up to make it a success, and religions were used to put fear in people, amongst many other strategies.

"Could it be possible that all those schemes turned into the politics that we vote for today? I think so. Suffice it to say that most of the policies of the wise ones are built on racist backgrounds, even though we say no to racism everywhere. The Africa leaders who knew the truth are prepared to keep quiet as long as they are bribed. Well, not just bribed! They also get the freedom to set their own Ponzi schemes and damage Africa even more! Are we ever going to talk about the elephant in the room, or are we going to continue to keep quiet and watch the world fall apart? People are not stupid; they know they are being finessed and patronised, but they are scared to talk. They are scared because of the situation around us, and fear is depriving them of their real freedom and liberty. It is okay for them to fear because they have lived in the world and they want to stay with loved ones for as long as possible. That gives leaders the temerity to continue to take people for fools."

He referred to the shout for equality as gimmicky when the policies make it look like it is okay to do bad things behind closed doors but not in public. One of the famous western immigration laws he said he found disturbing was when they tell foreigners to wait a minimum of six months to get a decision. He said they are not genuinely trying to help people. "In my opinion, it may be seen as a way to disorganise immigrants and try frustrating them back to their countries of birth. I think it is wickedness when applications are thrown under the desk and the authorities are seemingly waiting patiently for applicants to crack. The majority of applicants can't afford to live in that situation, and they go on the streets to beg for food and money. They even sleep on the street in the name of governmental policies. It is not a guess. I have been approached by these people for money several times on the street, and I was told to wait for that long a few times. I could feel the depth of these people's complications. Luckily for me, my survival skills, learnt from many years of gallivanting and the unity in my family, would not put me in a position to ask anybody for anything. I have lived in social housing where I could not afford electricity or gas; all I had was the light of my phone, and I always made sure the phone went off by the time I fell asleep in a cold flat. I would wake up, go to coffee shop, recharge my phone, and follow the same routine for days. But guess what? I never felt sorry for myself. I always found a way of moving forward. We can argue that I was not exactly walking or running, but I was crawling. Whatever the case may be, I still saw it as progress."

He maintained that it is baffling that when Africans see the so-called expatriates in their country, they start to prostrate and worship these expatriates like they are gods—and then when they go to these expatriate countries, Africans are referred to as illegal immigrants. "When I ran away from home with a map of the world in my hands, I started from the Republic of Benin , which shares a border with Lagos state of Nigeria. I crossed to Togo and then Ghana before getting stranded in Ivory Coast. I was a gullible and stupid young man who was under the impression that I could connect through the Ivory Coast to Agadez in Central Niger so that I could connect to Europe from there. I even ignored the early warnings whereby people submit to drinking their own urine. Despite the trouble I was in, I could not help but notice every African country I went to treated white people with superiority but treated fellow Africans like shit. It's safe to say people have been manipulated beyond control and are, as a result, still looking down on one another to date. In the African countries I travelled to, I heard people say, "Go back to your country. This is my country." Nothing was done about it because we are used to not respecting each other. It is absurd to see fake campaigns about equality when the wise ones are using it for propaganda. I am begging the wise ones to let my people go. I know this cannot be done overnight, but we need to start rewriting history and leave a positive stage for our future generations to play on. We were aware of UKIP Henry Bolton's partner, Jo Marney, making racial comments about Meghan Markle.

Lend me your ears, people. Before you get into a relationship with anyone, you go on dates to get to know each other. It is a slap on black people's faces for Henry Bolton to pretend he was not aware of how his fiancée felt about black people. In fact, I think that might be what they have in common and where their love chemistry started. To add insult to injury, he refused to step down as UKIP leader. If that does not mean that he endorsed his partner, then I do not see any other reason why he should still be there. Let's imagine for a second that the people of United Kingdom vote such a person to be prime minister. A lot of attacks would occur on ethnic minorities in the name of unjust policies and phoney laws."

He made it clear that we are being told indirectly that it is okay to be racist as long as it is done behind closed doors. He talked about his admiration for Prince Harry, who's always had my respect. He admires the bravery of this controversial prince, who felt the baritone of his voice may not be loud enough, and he did the extraordinary thing by choosing an African American for a fiancée. "Now that's how to live by example—not by wearing poppies and fake charitable acts. We black people need to wake up from our slumber and smell the coffee. Without love, the situation around the world will continue to go downhill. It is a very sensitive topic, but I am nostalgic about the melancholy behind what people of the world find acceptable. The wise ones need to start looking after foreigners in their own countries before travelling to do charity work in Africa. They have to stop meddling out of greed or selfish interests in order to make the globe more peaceful. Many people are rebelling against the pretentious behaviour of the wise ones, which is the reason we see different groups coming up and launching ferocious, deadly attacks against the wise ones. To people who feel hard done by, I advise you not to use terror for terror. Instead, respond with love; that way, they will feel stupid. Let's not succumb to stereotypes because that plays into their hands. We need to stick together and demand equality in a more civil way."

He classified religion as political, and he said something that I found mind-boggling. The fact that Jesus is portrayed to be white and Satan is portrayed to be black is not a coincidence! Thinking about it makes me think nobody really knows what's going on around the world. Personally, I think religion could have been used to capture and control people's mind. There is definitely a power up there, and I still call him God, but Alex and I share the same view: however anybody chooses to connect with God, it is not our place to judge. The judgement is with the creator of heaven and earth.

Alex feels religion is used as a Ponzi scheme. "How they are using religion to play people is worrisome. African leaders inherited the Ponzi scheme from wise men, from heartless people who have the effrontery to pick whatever chapter or verse in the Bible that can work to their advantage. Africans closed their eyes while the wise ones prayed for them, and by the time they opened their eyes, they got anointing and the holy ones got the land. The situation has evolved since then: the groomed African leaders fell in love with tithing verses in the Bible. It is like they are selling Christianity to people. I came across a story about one African governor who claimed that he used ten billion naira (£20m or $35m) to build a church! I can tell you this is money laundering. Ten billion naira will build eight to ten five-stars hotel, so unless the church was built with gold and diamonds, it is an insult to true lovers of God. What breaks my heart about the situation is that one the most respectable pastors in Africa was there to launch this crime called an international church. Our worldwide leaders need to pack it in and have a bit of respect for humanity. They need to stop selling people dreams and do the honourable thing. I can assure them that if greed could be set aside, then the world would be a better place."

Africa to Unite

When talking with Alex about Africa he said "we all know the horrors of slavery are too daunting to be overlooked. What makes the situation worse is the unperturbed and unremorseful manner in which imperialists are handling the situation despite it being the most inhumane crime against humanity. Let's drop religion and racial sentiment for a second and have a tête-à-tête about the truth, an objective argument that is healthy for the soul. The oppressed know they are being oppressed, and the oppressors know they are oppressing people in a subtle and tactful way. Everybody is operating with diplomacy. If the diplomatic approach was working, there would not be innocent people dying around the world. The brutality of mental slavery can lead to death through self-harming or mass murder. Political leaders need to start campaigning for true love interracially, or else things can get worse. The proceeds of the slavery business are used by colonial masters to buy allies amongst African leaders, and this is disgraceful. In short, it is disrespect to humanity! That money should be invested in campaigning for togetherness and youth empowerment because the youths are our only hope of a better tomorrow.

"There are many inconsistencies about religion that I find worrisome. It is the most effective weapon that was used to capture and regulate our thoughts for their selfish gain. I am sure most pastors and followers of God are not aware of King James being a British monarch was heavily involved in the slavery business. We all like to be strategic to help our business develop, and so I would not be surprised if the Bible was altered based on a conflict of interest."

The other thing Alex said that was really disturbing is both the oppressed and oppressors call on the same God! He said it does not make any sense for slaves and slave masters to call on the same God for prayers. He said he is very sure one is calling on God and the other is calling on the devil, because God is not in support of slavery. He said the last time he researched what religion stands for, he found out it may have been from the Latin verb *religare*, which means "to tie back; to thwart from forward progress; to bind; to hold back". "It's a system of control based on the unchallenged, dogmatic belief which holds back the progress of consciousness." He maintained that it is starting to look like this was done to African heritage to put fear in them with the belief that when they die suffering, they have a great opportunity to go heaven and enjoy, whereas the white man's heaven is here on earth.

He asked me candidly what happened to our story before the invasion, and if there was anything they were trying to hide from us. "They are clearly trying to tell us that a good slave is a good Christian!" He said if the Bible was adjusted by a British monarch like King James, no wonder you see quotes like this in the Bible: "Slaves, obey your earthly masters with respect and fear, and with sincerity of heart, just as you would obey Christ. Obey them not only to win their favour when their eye is on you, but as slaves of Christ, doing the will of God from your heart. Serve wholeheartedly, as if you were serving the Lord, not people, because you know that the Lord will reward each one for whatever good they do, whether they are slave or free"[12]

Alex hopes it is time for Africans to wake up from their sleep and demand answers! He believes togetherness of people from African heritage is a threat to the lies we were told for hundreds of years, and the wise ones see it as the reason they pretend to have our interests through Ponzi schemes and charitable aids, only for them to be in control of our minds and our freedom. "My ordeal in the hands of fellow Africans in the Ivory Coast helped me see how damaged Africans are. We are being insulted to our faces by portraying the devil as a black person and Jesus as white,

[12] Ephesians 6:5-9

yet we are trying to find out how they put fear and unrest amongst us. I am not sure whether I am the only person rethinking the story of Garden of Eden. The garden in question may have been Africa, and the snake that visited Adam and Eve may have been blue eyes and red face. The snake colonised Adam and Eve to cover their nakedness, and the intruders colonised African people to think the way they want us to think, putting what they want us to study in front of us so they can maintain their illusion of supremacy.

"When I arrived in the United States, the discrimination and inequality amongst people made me research the history of black and white people. I came across some uncanny stories that made me wonder whether it is possible for love to reign in the world. Black history has been completely wiped out! I do not know what happened to black history before the invasion in 1450 BCE. Egypt was said to be the most civilized country in the world throughout antiquity, and it was the dream place to be between seven and two thousand years ago. Why is such a story not in the history we studied in school? If imperialists were as superior as they claimed they were, why were they interested in Africa's resources? The level of terrorism made me dig even deeper into why Islamic groups are upset with white people to the extent that they do not mind killing themselves in the process of killing other innocent people. If people would agree with me, then the stigma of the disturbing slave trade, the most inhumane crime in history that happened hundreds of years ago, is not something that can be completely wiped out, but I believe people can make an effort to try if the accused are remorseful by embracing other cultures! I'm not talking about the charade some put up to deceive people that they are in support of equality. History proved that white men taught black people how to hate themselves. When I refer to black people, I am referring to black Africans, black Americans, and black Caribbean. We are all from Africa. I don't need to dig too far into how they find themselves wherever they live today. I was shocked when an African guy I play football with started mimicking the African accent. He got upset when I told him he hates himself and needs to educate himself more to understand that what he was doing was self-hatred. I told him that he might be traumatised from what he experienced in school, and he should get help by speaking with a professional. How could he disrespect the same accent that got him ready for school as a kid?"

The hard lesson of self-hatred is something that has to be tackled before the fight of equality can manifest. A child needs to learn to crawl before learning how to walk. The damage done is too ferocious to be ignored. By the way, I am trying to preach love as opposed to preaching hatred. I just feel that we need to touch the root of the problem for the opportunity to find a meaningful solution. Part of induced self-hatred is when they portray black people from the hood to be dangerous because they take a bit of cannabis and get hyperactive. When you hear news about someone being chopped to pieces inside a travel bag, or when someone is locked in a basement as a sex slave, the perpetrator is almost always white! So who is more dangerous? We need to remind our global leaders that greed is the root of all evil. Greed brought the missionary to Africa to brainwash people and make them slaves. It later stopped, but when foreigners go to western countries, they are referred to as immigrants—but when western people go to a foreign country, they call themselves expatriates. Does that sounds like equality? Of course not! There is still a lot of manipulation going on around the world, just for intruders to have access to the resources of different countries. If people were set free from the self-proclaimed superiority of colonial masters because they felt the like of black people were half human, then they should let them stay free.

Different interpretation of the stigma of racism is why there is unrest around the world today. We need to start campaigning togetherness and improve people's education all over the world to enhance a positive perception about right and wrong. Religion has been a weapon of manipulation up until today. King James I was the British monarch who took over when Elizabeth I passed on and his version of the Bible is the most respected in churches today. He supported slavery and lived his heaven here on earth. His family to date still gets paid for doing nothing at the expense of people. Can we trust such a person to tell us the truth about what God really stands for?

With much uncertainty about religion, the only visible gateway that can set us free is love! The Bible was said to play a major part in convincing people to get onto those slave ships. I saw a write-up where they said that black people were told to close their eyes, and by the time they opened them, white people had the lands and black people had Jesus. I do not want to talk too much about religion because I believe in God a lot and fear him to a fault. I fear God because of personal experiences and because I have a solid relationship with him. God is love! That is why I'm trying to let everybody know that love is all we need to correct what is going on around the world today. Meddling only worsens situations. We are left with more than enough to deal with in respect to our leaders in Africa. The induced self-hatred makes African leaders steal more than they can spend, and they end up keeping the money in western offshore accounts. These African leaders claim to be educated but lack the common sense to know that the money they steal and hide in foreign accounts is available to the foreign countries to use. That's the reason why there are no developments in the African country from which they stole the money.

Money laundering is going on in Africa through religious places. There are different pastors in Africa using private jets while people around them die in poverty. Some Christians might see this as blaspheming, but it is nothing like that. For example, the average monthly salary in my country of origin is around forty thousand naira, or the equivalent of one hundred dollars. Can someone tell me how it was possible to donate enough for pastors to get private jets?

Could the tithe be 10 per cent of stolen funds? After all, we have many top government officials who attend these churches, and if there is corruption all around Africa, then there could be crime in the churches. There is even this habit of church members donating to churches so that they can build schools, and church members cannot afford attend these schools because of how expensive the schools are. Who is fooling whom? We also have governmental organisations like the United Nations. Fela Anikulapo Kuti sang, "Who and who are unite inside United Nations?" Iraq against Iran. Syria against Israel, Palestine against Israel, Russia against America, North Korea against South Korea! Tell me the particular countries that are united within the United Nations. It seems to me that Ponzi schemes are ways to violate or manipulate people. What is the benefit of campaigning against racism when the system is saying otherwise? I saw a beggar on the street who said to me that immigration held on to his application for over six months, leaving him stranded. He could not work or get any form of income because he had been rendered useless. We have intelligent and educated leaders who would have anticipated such complications, but I do not think any of them care. It's fair to give a response to people on time, but it does not matter if the answer is yes or no. People should be put out of their misery rather than letting them wait for six months before they tell them no. This is still something that can enhance self-hatred. To me, this is still a display of superiority, even though it is not the same when western people visit or live in the country of these ethnic minorities and are referred to as expatriates.

If the government is not doing enough, then how can we rewrite history with love? Governments of western countries have to set examples regarding how to properly tackle the inequalities that are tearing the world apart. If people see that ethnic minorities are being treated with respect, then they will follow the footstep. We are all human beings, and no one should be made feel half-human. It baffles me when I see comments like this. We are living in the twenty-first century, and people don't understand how some vocal racists violate people of ethnic minorities! Are people being taught how to keep things quiet or how to live together in harmony? This is the reason I feel that we all have to search our hearts to see that life is short and that we should treat one another with love. I hope this raises awareness to Africans and other ethnic minorities to love themselves because charity begins at home. When there is self-love, it will make it easier for colonial masters to give them the respect they deserve.

In the Ivory Coast, Alex came across three Muslim brothers living together in one room. He said it would be bad of him to talk about the xenophobic attack he encountered and not talk about genuine love from fellow Africans who hailed from Burkina Faso. They took him to their home when they saw what he was going through. He stayed there for his last eight weeks in Ivory Coast. They prayed to Allah in one corner, and Alex prayed to God through Jesus in another corner. That is what I call unity. Religion should not hinder our love for one another. Everybody is trying to reach the big guy upstairs; he is strong, powerful, and immortal, and so nobody should fight his battles for him. He has the world on the tip of his finger. As for me, the world is my country and love is my religion. I do not care if you are Hindu, Buddhist, Christian, or Muslim. We all have to come together and rewrite history by letting the love flow. I hear people say that if they fight for their God and die in the process, they will go to heaven and have seven virgins! Has anybody been to heaven and back? People might feel upset about the history before them, but it is time to rewrite this history with love. The western governments have to help by being careful with their meddling. Alex said he will go back to Ivory Coast soon to find those three brothers. He will be looking to find out if things have improved there in regards to xenophobia. The situation in Libya, where the slave trade is said to still be going on up till date, was one of the reasons he decided to share his story for this book. It is important to let people know that if something is not done now, things can get worse. This xenophobia has been going on for decades; it was done behind closed doors because most of the victims were classified as illegal perpetrators. The offenders know the victim's high commission doesn't care about their citizens, only their pockets, so nobody can defend them.

Bereavement

Alex shared the heart-breaking story of losing his dad and little brother within 728 days. He described them as defining moments in his life. His life has not been the same ever since. He has since been scared of life and could not comprehend what coming to life was all about in the first place. The death of his brother was his first experience of losing a direct family member, and the matter got worse when he lost his dad just two years after.

"It was a Saturday morning. I had just woken up with a severe hangover when my phone rang. I was going to ignore it because I was still tired, but I managed to pick up the phone. On the other end of the phone was my mum, who sounded sober. She told me to pray so that my little brother would not die. I answered okay, and she dropped the phone. Then I remembered how religious my mum is. There was no way she would have told me to pray for him to not die if he was not dead already. I called my sister to ask what the problem was. My sister passed the phone to her husband, and he said my little brother was gone. I asked what he meant. Then my uncle grabbed the phone from him to tell me my brother had passed away! I screamed, and my hangover cleared. I could not cry but was in ferocious agony. I turned to booze, but it made the situation worse. When I got drunk, I blew every small thing out of proportion and carried out transferred aggression on petty matters.

"The death of my little brother was very disturbing for me, and I started to live in fear. I felt if death could take my kid brother, then it could take anybody at any time. I could not handle the stress and booked an appointment to speak with a therapist. It was really helpful but did not take away the pain and fear. At this point, I came to terms with the fact that it is something that will stay with me for the rest of my life, but I need to always think of my fond memories of him.

"After two years when I was just getting over my little brother's exit, Father passed as well!" He described his father's exit as insult to injury. Alex was broken and still remains confused today, but he made it clear he is fully determined to keep moving forward no matter what it takes.

"The whole family came together as one in our quest to put the disaster behind us. What made the situation with my dad worse was the fact that he was told he would die. It's even more painful trying to imagine what he was going through, knowing he was about to leave his family. He did something unusual by leaving some money behind for his own burial; he did not want to bother anybody with the expenses. Although I was upset he never said anything to us, at the same time I respect his bravery and determination to not get us too worried about his inevitable death. Father had a secret none of us knew about while he was living: we had a sister older than my other siblings and me. She showed up for his burial, and we were able to keep everything under control. I was amazed about how my dad could keep that story a secret for his entire life.

"After my dad's burial, things got more difficult. The hole my dad and kid brother left was never filled. The whole family didn't know how to handle the situation; we were short of words. We were all consoling each other. My dad never recovered from the death of my kid brother; he did not speak much, but the agony on his face was glaring."

Alex travelled back to America almost immediately after the burial. He was still drinking heavily to try to get over the ordeal. He attended the gym six days a week and saw a therapist for three months straight. His therapist encouraged him to go to the gym because he had picked the healthiest hobby, and she advised that he maintain his passion for gym because it was obvious. Although he could not come to terms with the bereavement of losing his father and his little brother, he always tried to not let anything disturb the fantastic memories he had of them.

"My best memory of my little brother was the day he got christened. He was only seven days old, and I held him in my hands. I didn't know how to feel as I was a young boy myself; I was joyful and scared at the same time. I was scared to drop him because he looked fragile and beautiful. My best memory of my father was when I was around the age of four. I faked malaria because I wanted attention, but I got more than I bargained for. He drove me to the hospital and carried me on his shoulder when we arrived there. The love I felt from him was worth me faking the illness, and the malaria injection I was given taught me not to use petty lies to get my way. We grow up learning from our parents and picking one or two lectures of our own along the way. My father and brother may have died physically, but they live in my heart."

Sex and Power

Alex had a severe problem with sexual addiction, and I applaud his bravery for being vocal about it. It is something he's not proud of, and he told me he has gotten help for the situation, which helped the therapist link it with the abuse he'd suffered at the age of nine, when he was taken advantage of by an older woman in her thirties. His therapist said he was overpowered because he was too young to make a decision regarding whether or not he wanted it. He started to have much meaningless coitus because he was subconsciously trying to get back his power that was taken from him at the age of nine.

Alex's self-awareness makes him to strive to be the better version of himself, which is the reason he's never shy to get necessary help when required. He never stopped researching how to overcome these obstacles to make sure he can relate with victims of similar abuse. He's raising awareness to make sure they don't live with such a burden that could deprive them of happiness.

I asked Alex if he was comfortable talking more about the actual abuse, and I asked for permission to write about it in this book. He agreed, hoping it would make an impact for people in similar situations to set themselves free. He further explained, "My urge for sex made me book myself for therapy. It was linked with my severe anxiety and abuse by older woman when I was the young age of nine. She took advantage of me as a little boy and had repeated coitus with me, telling me where to put it and instructing me to go up and down. People might argue that I shouldn't still remember exactly what took place, but I have to say that it was a proper sex lecture, and I still remember it in detail today. I didn't know what I was doing at the time, but I figured it out when I was around fourteen because that was when the penny dropped that I was having coitus. My quest to put what I'd been taught into practice was my focus at the time. It did not go well for me trying to find a girlfriend because I was a pale, big-headed little boy who got bullied by students from numerous schools and, painfully, girls' schools as well. You can imagine that no girl wanted to be associated with me because of people's impression about me. I wrote many love letters, sent multiple cards to people, and tried everything in my disposal to get a girl's attention, but it was not going to happen at that time. The urge to get laid intensified, and I spoke to one of my friends at the time, Peter. He advised me that the best thing to do was to pay for sex and get it over and done with. I agreed almost immediately and asked him to suggest a place to get the right prostitute. He did just that, and I was told I didn't do bad considering it was my consented first time."

He said that eased the urge for months—until it became a habit. He also mentioned the first girl he fell in love with, Catherine, because he didn't give up trying to find a proper girlfriend either. He lost his head the first time he set his eyes on her. He fantasised about her for couple of months before he could summon up the courage to talk to her. Her blatant response was no! That was the first moment Alex realised that he had a high level of perseverance. He kept presenting his case to her until she approved him with a condition. She said that being boyfriend and girlfriend didn't mean they could have sex. All he was allowed to do was endless kissing and making out, and he confirmed that was good enough because he loved her a lot. It did not take a long time before Alex fell in love with her. He said she made him feel like he was alive because she was his first love. He treated her with the utmost respect and worshipped the ground she walked on. He said there was a time he visited Catherine's house and her mum would be at work. Unluckily for them, her mum walked in on both Alex and Catherine making out. The moment Alex said hello to the mum and she walked into the kitchen, he scarpered, moving as fast as he could. But that could not stop a boy who has just fallen in love for the first time. They both continued with their love and exchanged many gifts.

Alex would later part ways with Catherine, she had gained admission to university before him and was able to meet different people and see different kinds of lifestyles. It was only a matter of time before he was binned. It was a difficult pill for Alex to swallow, but he had to move on because he felt inferior. He was under the impression that she had left him after gaining admission into a higher education institution while he was gallivanting and trying to be cool. A few years down the line, she got married, and they are still married today with kids. Alex went on to meet very few other girls and loved a couple more before he embarked on his world tour.

Alex later arrived in America, and he loved the country from the moment he stepped foot in it. He was stunned by the multicultural society. He could not help but notice the amount of pretty girls from different ethnic backgrounds everywhere he looked. The first thing he said to himself was, *This is home!* Alex met so many girls along the way who wore their hearts on the sleeves about their high sexual desires. There is this saying: "Real recognises real." He wanted a lady on the street and a freak in the bed. He went on to get all the freakiness he desired, from ménage à trois to sex parties. He had sexy women from all countries and races in the world. If Alex met great ladies but their sex drive was low, it made them incompatible. He said from experience that there are some women who can power your success, and there are some who can send you to your early grave. "What I am trying to say is either you get a lady or a freak. It is always difficult to get the one I desire: a lady *and* a freak! Just being a lady was not enough to spark my soul."

Alex went on to meet hundreds of women. He described himself as a rugged-looking guy who was always interested in pretty and glamorous women. He met quite a few of them who adored his level of intelligence mixed with my cool lifestyle. He tried all his life not to be dominated in the same way he was at age nine.

This went on for a long time until Alex met a Pakistani, Cuban, and Jamaican goddess. Alex said, She looked unbelievably beautiful, and he felt he was lucky that she wanted him. She said that she saw determination and perseverance in him, which made her give him a chance. They met through a mutual friend and were quick to go on their first date. He didn't know that he was setting up for a serious adventure. She made him wait three months before their first weekend together. They went back to his house, her first visit there, and they went straight to the bedroom. They danced to Jodeci and set the room on fire. Many guys would bring such a lady breakfast in bed, but Alex woke her up holding a magnum bottle of Dom Perignon, and she loved his concept. They finished the big bottle in a short period of time and went back to play. It was the first time that he responded eight times before it got dark. They didn't stop the day after either—she was with him from Friday night to Monday morning. All the food and drink that they needed was delivered to his door, and it didn't take long before they started a proper relationship.

"My relationship with her was non-stop fun and crazy drama. I loved it to a fault, and I loved her. She ticked all my boxes for my dream girl, but she was as crazy as me. It made it fun but brought conflicts. We had coitus everywhere from alleyways to cinemas. The girl looked stunning, the sex was on fire, and she was one thousand times a lady."

The conflicts between them increased because she had different ideas of what she wanted her partner to be. Alex was not allowed to talk back during arguments because she would call him a "nancy"! She said men could not talk back, but she'd rather wait for her partner to get her into bed and then pass his judgement as the king of the bed! She said that her boyfriend could beat her on the bed and do whatever he liked to her there. He thought she was joking until she tried to make him hit her, but he was not interested in doing that. There was a time that she busted his lower lip with a remote control, expecting him to beat her. He instead screamed at her, and the neighbours called the police. They asked if he wanted to press charges, but he was too shy to admit his girl had assaulted him, and he loved her too much to put her through that. It happened in her house, and so the police told him to leave and let it cool off for a day or two. He went across the road, hiding and waiting for the police to go. When they left, he went back and pressed the buzzer, and she said, "Is that you, Alex love?" He said yes, and she opened the door and tore off his clothes as soon as he entered her flat. They had erotic sex to make up, and she put his head back to where she wanted it.

It was fun for a while, but he could not take the pressure that came with it, and they decided to part ways. It was a bad breakup for him, and he subsequently turned back to his baby boy lifestyle.

At this moment, he felt he understood women more and was able to deal with what he described as the unpredictable side of women better than he used to. He went on to date many women, which increased his number of sexcapades, but he didn't use the word *love* often. He later met this lesbian stunner named Paulina. He said she fancied him enough to get intimate with him and be heterosexual for one night, and she told him after that it was a one off; she never entertained his future sexual requests. However, she remained in his life for years as his friend, and they both kept their little secret from everybody.

He remembered travelling back to Nigeria to sort his business. While he was in Nigeria, he met this police chief who had a fatal attraction for him. She was very generous to Alex and gave him everything. She insisted on being there for him financially because he was struggling a little bit. She wanted coitus as much as Alex did, and they even had coitus with her wearing her police uniform. She was confident that she owned him, and she tried to use voodoo to keep him under her control for life. Her voodoo failed, and he was shocked at the fact that she had the temerity to tell people that she'd tried voodoo on Alex and it never worked. She thought that Alex would blackmail her or sell her story because of her status, but little did she know that Alex doesn't kiss and tell."

Alex was able to reunite with Catherine. She was the girl who'd left him when they were teenagers. He did mention that she was his first love and his first rejection. He mentioned the fact that they didn't have proper coitus, and he gave up, thinking it might have to be the next world before it could happen. However, life has different plans for people, and their paths crossed again. She came to Nigeria at a time he was there. "Sex didn't come into my mind, but we found ourselves in a compromising position, and we finally made love. She was older but still stunning. I was ashamed of myself for succumbing to temptation. We reignited our childhood fantasy almost immediately, and we started proclaiming our love for one another. When it was time for me to travel back to America, Catherine changed her flight to enable her to travel the same day as me because she was due to travel back to England. We were inseparable, like teenage lovers, and we had sex at the airport, in a family changing facility. It was dangerous and we could have been caught, but that made the coitus more enjoyable. Although she travelled back to be with her husband and family in England, we had built a memory that will live with me until I die. I could have taken her from her husband, but I did not want to be selfish. I miss her and think about her a lot, but some relationships are too complicated to be considered."

Alex returned to America thinking about his life as usual, and he immediately arranged an appointment with a therapist. He wanted help on how to be happy and keep one proper relationship, and he wanted to find out why he felt the need to want to be intimate with many women. "My therapist told me that it was a power thing. She said that I felt overpowered by the devil that had stolen my youth at the age of nine years old, and she thought that it made me feel powerful to convince many women to open their legs and have coitus with me. It is delusional, however, because power can be very damaging. If the power I was trying to seek was helpful, I should have stopped thinking about the whole traumatising experience by now and had everything the way it should be. All I was doing, out of ignorance and a lack of self-awareness, before now was running away from a problem I should have faced head-on. I have since slowed down a bit, trying to find someone who can spark my spirit. My regret here is if Africans were more exposed and aware of mental trauma, I could have gotten the help I had always needed, and perhaps I could be happier now. Despite having coitus with many women, my mirror still reminds me that I am not happy, and so I have made up my mind to live with the traumatic experience until that one person comes forth to change my story. I hope to overcome my high sexual desire and focus on the cause of my high sex drive by learning from it and always being open to professional help."

Managing Anger

I was not too surprised when Alex told me about his bad temper. It's doesn't take a rocket science to know that his traumatic life experience would have triggered his temper. In fact, I'm surprised how that man is still standing and staying positive about life. He was cracking jokes, laughing, and staying optimistic about life and people. It is safe to say he is a mentally strong person and a certified force of nature. He said his temper was linked with him being bullied as a kid. He was apparently bullied in his school and in the city where he lived with his family. He dealt with it alone and without any conclusive solution. At the age of eleven, his confidence was already damaged, and he did not want to mix with other kids of his age. He had a habit of lashing out at his parents' property destroying things like electronics, plates, glasses, cups or any delicate thing around him when he got pissed off.

"I remember my parents always told me to take life easy, that life was not that serious, and that I shouldn't be screaming and destroying things. They said that people with aggressive anger issues tended to suffer a stroke or have a heart attack. I never paid attention because I was too stuck up to listen to my parents' advice. I wish I had been brave enough to tell them I was getting bullied not just in my school alone but all around the city in which we were living. There was a social book we used at the time to socialise across schools. It was called the slum book. How this book worked was you would write your name and details at the beginning, and you would also talk about your likes and dislikes, plus your relationship status. People would have to fill the whole exercise book by answering every question you asked them. I tried to socialise by getting involved and using slum book, not knowing I was making things worse for myself. The penny dropped when over 90 per cent of respondents gave a similar answer to my question, "What do you think of me?" My head was the focus of almost everybody! They compared my head to anything gigantic they could think of. I can't believe I am laughing now, because it was not funny at the time—it was very unkind and killed my self-esteem. My schoolmates were exchanging information with other secondary schools. I never knew the other schools had heard the horrible names they were calling me, but I realised the bullying and insults had gotten serious. I wept into my pillow many times without telling my family. I was clearly taking it out on my family by destroying things and making them sad."

Years down the line, he paid the price for not dealing with the situation the way he should have. He became overly defensive and was very quick to snap. It was so serious that he was sometimes referred to as a crazy person, despite how nice he tried to be to people. His anger overshadowed the positive perspective he deserved. He lost many people he cared about because when you are passionate about things you want and have a short temper, it's not always a good picture for people on the receiving end. "I think, generally, our mental health should not be taken for granted. Post-traumatic stress needs to be dealt with as we carry on with our journey in life. I have been in situations where people were genuinely joking with me, and I felt that they were just taking the piss out of me. In the process of displaying a bit of a tantrum, it became clear they were joking, and I would be too shy to stop the silliness I had gotten myself into. In the back of my mind, I would tell myself that it was not right to be feeling that way, and I still would not do anything about it and could land one in serious trouble."

Becoming a Father

One of the things I admire about Alex is the love he has for his daughter, although he has a tricky relationship with his daughter's mum and made it known that the daughter's mum does not exist in his head that hasn't stopped him from building his life around his daughter. He sees his daughter as his greatest achievement and is always striving to make sure her future is bright. "My daughter is my greatest achievement, but there have been tricky relationships between her mother and me, and this has caused tension between my daughter and me.

"I met my daughter's mum not long after I got to America. I was swept off my feet when I met young Tracy. The feeling was mutual about how we felt about each other. It did not take long before she was pregnant. I didn't know what to do because we were both young. I decided to break the news to my mum. Shockingly, my mum was okay with it; she said there was nothing wrong with it because kids are a blessing.

I was still panicking, but I decided that we would learn how to take care of the little one along the way.

"Nine months later, my daughter came along. I had mixed feelings. I was ecstatic and panicking at the same time. I panicked because I knew straightaway that I was responsible for another life, and I did not want to fail her. I remember when her mum delivered her at the hospital. They took her from her mum and gave her to me immediately. My hands were shaking, and I could not stop looking at her. The mum was in perfect condition as well, and she was discharged the same day. I called my family back in Nigeria to break the joyful news of my daughter's entrance, and everybody was happy about the new addition to the family."

After the first few days back home, reality started to kick in for Alex and his new family. The daughter's mum could not handle bringing her up. He had to go out and do some odd jobs to keep his daughter and the mum happy. However, he started to notice that his daughter's mum was not able to cope with the constant crying, the changing of nappies, and the sleepless nights that come along with a new born. If Tracy's mum was around, he could have suggested Tracy take his girl there, but her mum had passed away before Alex met her. Alex had to step up, trying to do the necessary things himself because it was both of their responsibility. It became extremely difficult because Alex needed to get his working hours in so he could get on the payroll and support his family. It got to a stage that Alex could not take it anymore, and he decided to get help from his mum in Africa. No member of Tracy's family wanted to know, apart from the granddad and his white English wife, Anabel (he had gotten married to Anabel after divorcing Tracy's grandma). I could understand why that had happened because she was not an easy person to deal with. She insulted Alex continuously and referred to him as "fucking African". Alex asked Tracy why the grandma was like that, considering the fact that she was also black, but she never had an answer for him.

One of Tracy's aunties, Elizabeth, supported her when she could. "I appreciated her because I knew that everybody has their own problems to deal with. It was at this point that I suggested we travel to visit my family in Nigeria. I knew that if I told her of my intention to let my mum look after her for a while, she would say no because people would discourage her from doing so if there was an iota of inclination. We got to Nigeria on holiday, and I made my intentions clear to her. She agreed with me because I said it was going to be for three months, and she saw I was from a good background. My family was very good with my daughter."

Alex and Tracy got back to America, and things got worse between Tracy's family and Alex. He said, Tracy's uncle, Zach, came to the house and ordered that he stay away from her. Out of respect, Alex did as he was told and left. They didn't get back together, which made Tracy put more pressure on Alex to bring their daughter back from Nigeria. Alex refused to do that because he was worried she was still not ready to take on a major responsibility like that, but she insisted that he bring her back or else she would take him to court. He refused and was told by the authorities to attend court and give his account of the accusation against him. The judge made it clear that neither Alex nor Tracy had a right to do that, and he was given seven working days to bring her back from Nigeria. He didn't have money to do as he was told at the time. He told the court about his lack of funds and was stunned by their intention to pick up the bill. His daughter's mother travelled to Nigeria, and his family emotionally handed his little girl to her after two years. She came back to America, and was denied access to her for years. His daughter's mum got married and started a new life. After some time, she had a change of heart and let him see his daughter from time to time.

Alex and Tracy maintained this arrangement for years, and Tracy never once mentioned to Alex that there was any form of a difficulty between them, even though she could see signs of rebellious behaviour. I guess she did not want to be branded a failure by Alex or a member of Alex's family, and she decided to keep it quiet. The mum panicked by the time the daughter was twelve years old and told Alex eventually what was really going on. She was not listening and was threatening to hurt herself. They both agreed this time around that it was in the interest of everybody that she goes back to Nigeria. Tracy and Alex could not travel at the time due to busy schedules, and they decided to make a special arrangement for her to go alone.

Both Alex and Tracy took her to the airport, and she was handed over to the airline. Alex family was waiting for her on the other side. She was there for three years, and they got updates from Alex's mum throughout her stay in Nigeria. She gave everybody a tough time, but Alex's mum was up to the task. She was in a private school throughout with close monitoring, and both her mum and Alex picked up the bill. She wanted to come back desperately and blackmailed her mum into bringing her back. She accused the mum of hating her and abandoning her in Africa as a result. The mum insisted that she come back, and Alex did not have any option but to give in to the idea.

"She came back and waited to turn sixteen before starting full-blown trouble. Her social worker and school got me involved, but we could not rescue the situation. The relationship between her, her mum, and the stepdad got out of hand, and she was kicked out of the house by her mum. She moved to my house but never liked it, thinking it was too boring and I was too strict. As a result, she forced her way into living at Elizabeth's place because she had a daughter who was the same age. Elizabeth was not ready to take her, but she could not do anything because my daughter refused to leave the house. She has being living there since, and I try my best to give any support within my ability, hoping she will grow up to see life is not a bed of roses."

Baptism

Football is one of the exercises Alex uses to keep fit. He would travel around the United States just to participate in footie exercise. He was later introduced to this church team, where he played on the amateur league for them. The whole concept of the church having a team was for evangelism, and they used it as a form of fellowship. He was dedicated and excited to wake up at 6:30 a.m. on Saturdays to partake in something he described as food for his soul. It helped him to stay focussed mentally when he got in his exercise or training. It was a matter of time before the inevitable happened: he was invited to church by the team to fellowship with the church he represented on the football field. It was a warm welcome for him as expected, and Alex would go on to attend the church every Sunday.

"It felt lovely to join this church, and I count myself lucky to be part of this Godly family. I attended every Sunday for almost a year and then decided to get baptised there. It became a regular thing for me to go to Sunday services until I was not so sure about religion. The confusion got me to do a lot of research in order to understand more about religion in general. I see a lot of violence in the name of religion, and I could not comprehend how some religions can disrespect God so much to think that he can't fight his own battles, and so they decide to fight on his behalf. When I hear extremists say they want to die for God so they can have virgins waiting for them in heaven, it makes me sad.

If anybody had gone to heaven and then come back, I would understand, but the level of manipulation around the world is eating away at us and tearing us apart. My experience in the Ivory Coast with the three Muslim brothers shows that there is space for all religions to play. They didn't have a problem with me trying to reach God through Jesus in their little room at the time, and I never had a problem with them praying to Allah. Call him Allah or God—there is only one God, and his mercy endureth forever.

"What scares me about Christianity is the history of how colonial masters used it to manipulate Africans. I mentioned earlier that some chapters and verses in the Bible instruct slaves to obey their slave masters. I do not care what anybody says; the God whom I know and have rapport with would not encourage cruelty and slavery to be a normal thing. I started to think about all this, and it got me confused about religion. Africans and other countries were kept captive even though they were said to have gained their freedom. How can you be free if you have been terminally brainwashed and the proceeds of slavery are on display without any remorse? We all have to search our hearts deeper to find the real love that can make the world a better place for us and generations to come. That moment you start emotionally clinging to your religion to the extent that truth and justice become secondary considerations, your education and exposure are useless. You need to be able to think beyond silly sentiments in order to avoid being a liability to humankind. We have to let love reign and allow room for everybody to practice the religion in which they believe. We all serve a powerful God, and he can fight his own battle.

"Greed is the problem behind people who turned religion into politics in order to power their own selfish gains. It is the same greed we see in churches today where some pastors use the church to extort Christians. We have seen predators who pretend to be clergyman. We have seen situations in Africa where pastors have lied and said that God asked them to put their hands into females' private parts to help them conceive."

Alex travelled to Nigeria for a few months when he was putting together his hotel project. He was really confused at seeing card payment machines amongst churches. He complained about it to people around him, but their responses showed it needed divine intervention to set their people free. No one saw anything wrong with it. "These machines are named Point of Sales. I remember I came across a verse in the Bible where Jesus instructed people not to turn God's house into a market. (John 2:16) I needed someone to tell me why there were business card machines in churches! The most common one is the tithe. We have seen a case of a government worker in Nigeria who paid millions of dollars in tithes, and her wages over the last ten years did not add up to two hundred thousand dollars! It was established by the Economic and Financial Crimes Commission (EFCC) in Nigeria that the woman donated the proceeds of crime to the church. Many governmental bodies see churches as safe ways to clean their money. There should be compulsory due diligence for experts in churches and other religious houses all over the world. I don't want to go too much into politics or professional careers, but close monitoring is essential with all religious places to combat money laundering and keep the world safe."

Alex stopped attending the church where he was baptised for a bit and was confronted by many church members asking if the pastor had said something that had put him off. He said it was never a personal thing between him and the pastor or the church; it was something he had to do for humanity. "There is too much unrest around the world. We have to individually and collectively search for that love that has been missing for hundreds of years. It started before and after the famous invasion that the stigma has left many of us scarred. It has left many deluded that there is even an iota of superiority from one race to another. It is very delusional for some barbaric people to still claim, in this day and age, that one race is better that another race. If anybody can live forever, then I will deem that person superior to me! There has been a name that history told us was talked about since the beginning of this world, and that name is God. That's the only supreme and immortal personality that I know and respect from the bottom of my heart. I reckon everybody should find their way of connecting with him and looking up to him as the author and the finisher of life. When you are connected to God, then you might not need a mediator to pass your message to him. He made eyes so he can see, he made ears so he can hear, he made brains and knows your tricks, and he made noses and can smell that stinking habit. From the little I know about this famous God, love is all we need to set us all free."

Alex has since started going to church again and even works as an usher in the church. I asked him the reason behind sudden change of decision, and he said he decided to attend again because of the bond between him and the church family. It was at this time that he started to see the true leadership of the pastor of the church. He said the pastor preaches in a way that one can tell he is not out there to judge anybody, and he does not make offering or tithing his focus. He explained further that the pastor set up the church in a way that one can feel genuine love, and he always emphasises that it isn't by force to donate in church. He encourages people to do so only if it comes from their hearts.

The Geezer in the Mirror

Alex still faces trauma and challenges describing his fear as being "So scared of the dark cloud blocking my view. It makes me wonder if the view is ever going to be clearer. I'm so worried about what is going to become of me. Favouring happiness over material things should be the easiest thing to achieve, but the twisted world has made happiness almost impossible. One minute you are in form and feel on top of the world, and next minute everything comes crashing down around you. The zigzag gesture you get from that bitch of a life makes one wonder: Would I die unhappy, or would I be lucky enough to get the fairy-tale happiness in my lifetime? I'm not supposed to be scared of my shadow, but it does frighten the living daylights out of me. The only person so far who understands me is the geezer in the mirror. I do wish the geezer in the mirror can advise me rather than just staring at me, but it would be the beginning of insanity. I tried many times to use financial achievements as a surrogate for happiness, but our hearts always have different plans. I will continue to stand up to the battles because I will never underestimate the danger of a low mood. I always try not to look past twenty-four hours ahead because it is a valid trigger of anxiety. I try to take every day as it comes and keep praying to always win the daily battles with my mind, because if the day wins over me, there might be no tomorrow. The baby inside me, my heart, is my priority, and I owe it a duty of care to delicately look after the baby to the best of my ability because it begets self-love."

Alex has come to conclusion, based on pleasant and unpleasant experiences, that winning does not mean there are no failures ahead and that failure does not mean there are no spectacular successes ahead. His willingness to share what he experienced shows his mental strength. He felt he learned something new about life in 2018 that makes him hell-bent to train his mind because he strongly agrees with the philosophy of mind over emotions. Life will not stop for anyone regardless of the situation, and hence he feels people always have to move forward because stopping would significantly alter one's life.

From the beginning of 2018 to the beginning of summer, he went through difficulties that made him understand why it was possible for people to commit suicide. However, he made it clear it was never an option all his life because of the fear of the unknown on the other side, and he would never want to hurt his loved ones. Alex was super low and felt empty; despite his achievements in life, he still feels they are all meaningless if one is not happily married with children. He said the institution called marriage has been in shambles in the last decade and a half. "It seems you have to be stupid as a man to make the institution marriage possible, especially in the western world, because men's emotions are never valid in the world we live in today. If you show too much emotion, the perception is always stupidity." He was also trying to facilitate some life-changing deal with his business, and he was distracted. Negative thoughts used this advantage to visit him, but he never stopped fighting.

He became confused about how prayer works as panic kicked in already. On a summer day 2018, before Alex went to bed, he went on his kneels to pray even though he had since stop praying. Call it coincidence, but Alex called it divine intervention from the big guy upstairs as Alex woke up to a call that changed everything around. His business deal has been concluded, and immediate payment was made to his account. He embraced his new change of circumstances and felt on top of the world, as if the mood had been lightened immediately. He would soon meet a Mexican girlfriend, Adonia, whom he'd adore so much. Adonia means beautiful in Spanish—no wonder Alex described her beauty as dangerous! Alex thought he had gotten everything he needed, but disappointment was waiting ahead.

Alex and Adonia split on suspected background incompatibility. They shared so many philosophies of life, and everybody could notice the chemistry. The one negative thing which proved costly enough to lead to their splitting up was they were both suffering from possible PTSD based on past experiences. It was a matter of time before this raised tension. Alex and Adonia soon made the decision to go their separate ways. Although Alex kept his head up, he is hoping he can work on improving himself and get ready for what the future holds. "If you noticed the swift change in my circumstances, then you will understand why I think it's always best to not think too much ahead. Worrying has never solved any situation, and panicking does not make things better. On the contrary, it is very unhealthy and can damage you or damage your happiness."

He believes life is a never-ending rollercoaster. The people who appear to be the strongest are also the weakest. Emotions have no boundary and do not understand how powerful or wealthy you are. The heart wants what it wants! A few bad chapters in our lives do not mean your story is over, even if your story is beautifully written with tenacity, self-belief, optimism, and most importantly love. In death your story may not be over because your legacy can still speak a billion words. This man's understanding about life and constant desire to master himself deserves a round of applause. He believes many people want to be happy even though they don't know how to be happy. They are so used to not being happy because they focus more on what's going wrong in their lives and forget to be thankful about what's going splendidly in their lives.

Pain

This topic reminds me of one of my favourite quotes ever, by John Muir: "Nature is ever at work building and pulling down, creating and destroying, keeping everything in whirling and flowing, allowing no rest but in rhythmical motion, chasing everything in endless song out of one beautiful form into another."[13]

Pain is a friend you don't want, but it always finds a way to be in your life, and there is nothing more difficult than trying to encourage the guy in the mirror when he is in pain. I know people wish they never experience pain or unhappiness in their lifetimes, but it is inevitable. It could be at work, it could be saying goodbye to people you have shared some fantastic experience with, it could be inflicted by discrimination, it could be betrayal, it could be bereavement—it goes on and on. What makes the situation more daunting is you have to keep up appearances when

[13] John Muir Quotes. (n.d.). BrainyQuote.com. Retrieved April 9. 2019, from BrainyQuote.com Web site: https://www.brainyquote.com/quotes/john_muir_7526891

life happens; your behaviour has to be acceptable to people who may not know the burden on you or the heavy load you're carrying in your mind. No matter what your circumstances are, you are responsible for your behaviour and your sanity. You can never let yourself go; when you drop on the floor, you have the capacity to bounce right back up, or you can make the decision to stay on the floor, broken. Your friends let you down, and your partner betrayed you. Even your family can betray you. Boohoo! Always remember to collect knowledge and wisdom to take learning from your failures and painful experiences.

We live in a world where you are told what to eat, whom to date, how to disrespect your parents, when to kick your husband or wife out of the house, how to be confused with your gender and defy biology, and what to accept and not accept from people. People are being confused left and right, and they can't differentiate right from wrong anymore. The wrongdoings look perfect in the world we live in today, and the right things seems inane and psychotic. Why is the situation like that? The foundation of this superficial world is built on lies and deceit through manipulation and conflict of interest. Politics has turned to cancer because they always find a way through institution to keep us captive. This has cost too much unrest around the world that people's brains find it difficult to process. People are anxious, depressed, suicidal or living in fear. People might not understand the link between what we go through and politics.

Alex shared one of his tantalising, unique life stories about a Filipino he saw for a few months, Rosamie. The girl had everything going on for her but permanently lived in fear. She had a traumatic experience on a holiday where she witnessed a terrorist bomb go off. She refused to seek professional help but felt everybody was out to get her. The situation got worse: she panicked and shook when unexpected things happened around her, she refused to get help. The situation started to affect her relationship with Alex. She was always anxious and panicking that a relationship with a potential fairy-tale ending would end unexpectedly.

In my view, political sentiments and manipulation cost terrorists a pain so that they feel revenge is the only way to heaven. Terrorists' revenge has cost Rosamie pain, and Rosamie's pain cost Alex the pain of losing someone he cared about so dearly, Alex said "she was red, and she liked me because I was blue. She touched me, and I became a lilac sky. She decided purple just wasn't for her." Alex handled the situation badly by making things worse because of his severe anxiety. It does not take a genius to know it is a chain reaction, and it will always drag people into uncanny negative energy going on around the world. He didn't let it disrupt his happiness by facing the situation head-on.

When the government creates a better option for women to have better lives without their husbands or their partners, then the option is subconsciously at the backs of their minds to kick their husbands out for situations that can be spoken about and used as a lesson to strengthen their union. Kids grow up without fathers, and some don't take long to join gangs and start carrying knives and guns. The death toll of young people being stabbed and killed has risen significantly, as result causing pain for victims' families and strangers who witness traumatic scenes. That can affect their mental health moving forward. We are all in this messed-up world, and it is imperative that we engage the root of the matter before an iota of positive outcome can be seen. Lower-class people and ethnic minorities are victimised to back up the psychotic lies that were told about humanity. Almost every leader in the world today has a negative motive to govern people. Some leaders want power so they can abuse it, some want money they don't need, and some simply want to maintain the status quo of delusional superiority. Humanity is doomed as a result of all these petty sentiments, and money has become the primary source of happiness for everybody. Yes, money does carry its weight when needed, but it does not bring happiness. Money was created for political reasons. I wonder how our forefathers got by without the introduction of money. It was introduced to distract people from finding out what their real purpose for living is. I've always said if you can't use your money to clone yourself, if you can only sleep in one room at a time in your big mansion, if your money can't buy you good health when you are terminally sick, and if your money can't buy you a wife or husband to truly love you, then money shouldn't be chased. But our quest for happiness, love for humanity, cherishing, and accepting people around us should be on top of our priorities in life.

A lot of induced pains are strategically and maliciously placed on people by lawmakers. It feels normal to us because they have successfully manipulated people all over the world. Alex said to me he does not think anybody is normal, and I kind of agreed with him. "The universe is in a state of confusion. We were taught subjects like biology growing up, and you will agree with me that biology is one of the most important subjects in school because it elaborates on our existence. The same biology was altered the moment there were bills passed that men are allowed to be women and women are allowed to be men. I am not trying to judge anybody because it isn't my place to judge, but things like this make a mockery of what we were taught in school. School is an institution, and so is government. Is biology right, or is the law right to defy biology?" That remains a big question that no one has an answer for—hence the confusion. The manipulation around the world is daunting and worrisome. Alex said "The damage goes deeper than what we see in front of us every day. I think ethnic minorities may have subconsciously come to terms with being inferior. Psychological attack has made many ethnic minorities grateful for any petty favours channelled their way strategically, and they may have settled as a result. It is not a mistake that you wear black to funerals and white to weddings. It is not coincidence that the devil was described as a black man and Jesus is white. It is not accidental that they blacklist debtors, and it's never a mistake that ethnic minorities are immigrants and Caucasians are expatriates."

Pain has become our friend because it was created amongst people who should be protecting our interests. The races have lost their identities because they are now following trends that were induced by selfish interests. Those who are not following the trend are setting the trend, and maintaining status quo is equally as draining as following the trend. The world is in disarray and could even get worse. People are kept busy with uncountable distractions around us, distractions are in our face every day, media is controlled with politics, food that can kill us are bestsellers in the society, and poisonous food owners are generating profits at the expense of humanity. People who are meant to protect us are giving windows to poisonous food sellers.

Self-love can get us through anything. You have to love yourself in order to love others. You have to search for inner peace, and then you will be more thankful for what you have and stop getting angry about the luxury you don't have. Stay away from distractions even though that is extremely difficult. It is difficult because media is all around us. Television tells you what is right and wrong in relationships, radio tells you about your ideal kind of partner, newspapers tell you when to use your hands to destroy the happiness you have built in your marriage, and social media sets unrealistic expectations and standard. What about the most important person? You! Are your thoughts influenced by what you see around you? What people do you take advice from? Are you taking advice from people who have failed perpetually in the task on which they're advising you? Recognise your instinct when the vision pops up and follow it through with calculated mission. Alex was discouraged and laughed at about business decisions that would go on to be his life security and his best financial achievement so far. People laughing at him were quick to congratulate him when the business delivered. Find your path in life, follow your instinct, take the calculated risk, and stick with what you believe in. I promise you can and will do it!

Conclusion

To conclude I go to Alex's words as they so beautifully capture the essence of this story and the lessons to learn.

"I feel like I'm living proof that God exists! My roller-coaster life story is very captivating; it shows life is full of endless battles. Your character needs to be on the stronger side. People are often broken because they lack character and the mental strength to withstand the inevitable testing periods we come across. Sometimes it could be negative occurrences that captured their youth. Too many people are knowingly and unknowingly suffering from post-traumatic stress because of what they went through in the past. People often think that those with drastic, obvious, erratic behaviour are the only people with mental challenges. There is some post-traumatic stress that affects our day-to-day activities and our relationships with people. Madness is not just when you take your clothes off or eat from the garbage can; a negative or edgy response to minor things can be as a result of your mental state. If we are more cautious of our mental state and get the necessary help needed from time to time, we will know how to handle it and make sure it does not hinder the goodness around the corner. Also remember that you cannot recover from anxiety by simply staying calm, and you cannot recover from anorexia nervosa by being a glutton. If mental health was that simple, we would not be struggling in the first place.

"As for upcoming teenagers, do not run away from home unnecessarily because you get excited by the love from our parents, thinking life is a bed of roses. It is very dangerous out there, and risking your life for no reason is not the wisest idea. I remember meeting a young teenager in the Ivory Coast. He came to the country with the intention of being a professional footballer. I guess he thought there was genuine love around the world, and it would only be a matter of time before he kick-started his football career. When he showed up at the barbershop, he saw kids playing football outside and borrowed the ball from them to freestyle. I have to say he was a good footballer. However, he continued with his journey to the main city of the Ivory Coast, and we didn't see him for two to three weeks. By the time we saw him again, he had lost his mind. He didn't know who we were anymore and was begging for food on the street. He had a big plate in his hand, and he was using his hand to describe to people that he needed food. Looking back at the situation, it was obvious that the situation was a bit too much for him, and the fact that he could not speak French made things worse. That made him lose his mind and use gestures to communicate with people in the country. We have to agree that the combination of begging on the street and gesticulating would not be looked at as the actions of a sane person.

"Unfortunately, I did not see the guy again until I left the Ivory Coast. I'm sure if God saw him through that, he would be asking himself now what he was thinking to embark on a journey like that at a very young age. I am not saying people feeling bullish about life like me should not play or do what they believe in, but it is rough, deadly, and dangerous out there. The worst has to be anticipated, and you have to be mentally ready for it. This is not a story to make Ivory Coast people look bad because I met some lovely people as well. I'm hoping it can raise awareness about how primitive and barbaric we can be in Africa, based on the trauma with which we are living. The stigma of colonial invasion is traumatic; people might argue that it happened to the early generations in Africa and that we should not be affected by it, but thinking of the direct aggression to our forefathers and the ongoing systematic invasion by wise ones is unacceptable.

"We have to settle with the past and engage with the future. We are Africans, we are the oppressed, and we should stick together and find a way to unite. If we stay divided, the wise ones are going to use us against each other. The most powerful tool in life is our brains; we need to seek knowledge and understand that we opened our doors to enemies, and it is high time the door is shut. If a thief has no intention of robbing you and sees your door open, the thief would enter because stealing is a habit for him. I believe that the majority of these wise ones have no interest in manipulating Africans anymore, but we have greedy leaders in Africa who are stealing more than they could spend in their lifetimes, and they are keeping the stolen money in the wise ones' countries. The money they pile away in offshore accounts is out of Africa and of no use to Africans; it is still empowerment for colonial masters. People may ask how this is possible, but banking is a way of lending a bank your money without cash interest. The only interest you get on your money is duty of care! Banks get the opportunity to use your money to generate interest at your expense. The country in which the bank is located is one of the beneficiaries of your funds. Many African leaders die, and nobody gets to claim their money from these foreign banks. The western countries are getting better day by day, and African countries are still getting extorted. The oppression and the damage caused to us Africans are so ferocious that we hate ourselves. Unless there is unity in Africa, the wise ones will not know how to stop their stylish invasion. A kid who raises his or her hands is the one the mother would carry. Let us educate one another and recreate history with love.

"The education I'm talking about is not to collect big academic titles and forget the main reason behind the education. We have too many educated illiterates in Africa who get accolades for prestige and approval in society. That's the reason most Africans like all these religious and academic titles. You hear engineer this, nurse that, alhaji this, and pastor that. When you are called alhaji in Africa, for example, people forget it is a title which is originally given to a Muslim person who has successfully completed the trip to Mecca. Suffice it to say that the real meaning of alhaji is stranger. Fela Anikulapo Kuti said this when I was much younger, and I never thought in a million years that what he was saying would be clearer as I got older: Knowledge is power. It is therefore imperative to gain this knowledge and use it properly rather than wasting it for the sake of future generations."

